THE COMPLETE FILMS OF
WILLIAM POWELL

THE COMPLETE FILMS OF

WILLIAM POWELL

By Lawrence J. Quirk

A CITADEL PRESS BOOK

PUBLISHED BY CAROL PUBLISHING GROUP

ACKNOWLEDGMENTS

Special thanks to Douglas Whitney, as always, for his generous loan of many rare and valuable stills and other photographs of William Powell. Also thanks to Ernest D. Burns of Cinemabilia, Inc., New York; Mark Ricci and The Memory Shop, New York; Jerry Ohlinger's Movie Material Shop, New York; Mary Corliss and the Photo Archives of the Museum of Modern Art, New York; Terry Geesken, Museum of Modern Art; Phototeque; British Film Institute, London; Dorothy Swerdlove, Dr. Rod Bladel and the staff of the Billy Rose Theatre Collection of the New York Public Library (film and theatre divisions), Library and Museum of Performing Arts, New York; Kirk Crivello, Bob Board, Myron Braums, Ben Carbonetto, Manuel Cordova, Bob Harman, Eduardo Moreno, John W.M. Phillips, and Lou Valentino, also to various personnel and friends at such companies as Metro-Goldwyn-Mayer, Warner Bros., Paramount, RKO General, Twentieth Century-Fox, Universal, United Artists and others who, without wishing to be named, kindly shared with me their personal and professional memories of Mr. William Powell.

Thanks also to James E. Runyan, William Schoell, Michael Ritzer, Arthur Tower, Doug McClelland, Albert B. Manski, Mike Snell, Don Koll, John Cocchi, Jim McGowan, Romano Tozzi and John A. Guzman, and the James R. Quirk Memorial Film Symposium and Research Service.

First Carol Publishing Group Edition 1990

Copyright © 1986 by Lawrence J. Quirk

A Citadel Press Book
Published by Carol Publishing Group

Editorial Offices
600 Madison Avenue
New York, NY 10022

Sales & Distribution Offices
120 Enterprise Avenue
Secaucus, NJ 07094

In Canada: Musson Book Company
A division of General Publishing Co. Limited
Don Mills, Ontario

Queries regarding rights and permissions
should be addressed to: Carol Publishing Group,
600 Madison Avenue, New York, NY 10022

Manufactured in the United States of America
ISBN 0-8065-0998-8

10 9 8 7 6 5 4 3 2

Designed by A. Christopher Simon

LIBRARY OF CONGRESS CATALOGING-IN-PUBLICATION DATA

Quirk, Lawrence J.
  The complete films of William Powell.

  1. Powell, William, 1892-1984—Criticism and
interpretation. I. Title.
PN2287.P58Q57   1986   791.43′028′0924   86-13646
  ISBN 0-8065-0998-8

Dedicated to the Memory of My Uncle

WILLIAM P. CONNERY, JR.

(1888-1937)

ACTOR   •   MEMBER OF CONGRESS

*Who played with William Powell in stock
in the long-ago*

CONTENTS

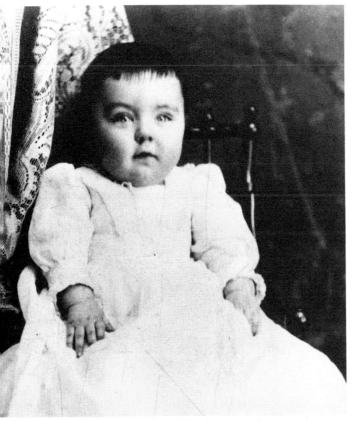

At age three months, 1892.

WILLIAM POWELL: THE ACTOR AND THE MAN

William Powell was Hollywood's most underestimated actor.

Although he had graduated from the American Academy of Dramatic Arts in 1912, and over the next ten years had played over 200 stage roles, including Shakespeare and the classics, and although in 95 movies between 1922 and 1955 he had taken on, and implemented with thoroughgoing professionalism, a startling variety of character types, he is still best remembered as the sophisticated playboy detective, replete with charm, poise and ineffable elegance, who teamed with Myrna Loy in six *Thin Man* films, and as the dapper, brittle Philo Vance of four earlier movies made from S.S. Van Dine mystery tales.

Yet it has not been sufficiently noted that he was nominated for Academy Awards three times, in 1934, 1936 and 1947, and that in the last year he won The New York Film Critics Award for his sterling portrayal of the formi-dable, crusty but deeply human paterfamilias Clarence Day in *Life With Father*.

During the 1920's, his first decade in films, Powell was one of the nastiest of cads and most sinister of villains in countless movies in which he supported personalities of far less talent than his own, who were largely to fade out with the advent of sound, whereas for him, sound was to be just the beginning of major success. When, in 1928, his superb speaking voice was impressed on the fans in one of the first ground-breaking talkies, *Interference,* he dramatically metamorphosed, in what seemed no time, into one of the most romantically delightful of male film stars.

As the talkie years proceeded, Powell demonstrated remarkable characterizational range—from the British Army officer in *The Key* to the governor in *Manhattan Melodrama* to the secret operative in *The Emperor's Candlesticks* to the gay comedian of *Love Crazy* to the jealous astronomer husband of Hedy Lamarr in *The Heavenly Body* to the amusing *Mr. Peabody*, who loved mermaid Ann Blyth, to the bumbling, venal lawmaker of *The Senator Was Indiscreet* to the world-weary but pixieish "Doc" of *Mr. Roberts*.

He appeared opposite some of the most noted female—and male—luminaries of the screen—thirteen times with Myrna Loy, twice with Hedy Lamarr, three times with Luise Rainer, three times with Carole Lombard (who was to be the second of his three wives), and with such as Kay Francis, Irene Dunne, Ruth Chatterton, Ginger Rogers, Jean Arthur, Rosalind Russell, Ann Harding, Joan Crawford and Jean Harlow, one of the great loves of his life, with whom he did two films.

Spanning as he did the decades from the Twenties to the Fifties, he started out opposite such silent stars as Bebe Daniels (they were for a while a popular teaming in the 1924-29 period), Lillian and Dorothy Gish, Marion Davies and Evelyn Brent, and toward the end wound up opposite Angela Lansbury, Esther Williams, the young Elizabeth Taylor, Lauren Bacall and Marilyn Monroe.

At age 22 in 1914 while in stock in Portland, Oregon.

Early in his film career.

He also either buddied with, or sinisterly opposed, a host of male co-workers over those 33 years, from John Barrymore to Richard Barthelmess to Ronald Colman, Gary Cooper, Emil Jannings, Clark Gable, Spencer Tracy, Robert Montgomery, Henry Fonda, James Cagney and Jack Lemmon.

He even got around to Bette Davis, in *Fashions of 1934*, a once-only pairing in which their distinctive styles and chemistries met, or rather, collided, for forgettable results. He worked over the years with many of the great directors, all of whom seem to have held him in great respect and esteem, including John Ford, W.S. Van Dyke (his *Thin Man* director), Mervyn LeRoy, Jack Conway, William K. Howard, Irving Pichel, Michael Curtiz, Victor Fleming, Gregory LaCava, Josef Von Sternberg and Henry King.

By no means conventionally handsome by Hollywood standards, Powell developed during the 1930's into one of the most romantically compelling of male stars, and one of the most highly paid. The arch-villain Tito Melema who menaced the hapless Lillian and Dorothy Gish in the 1924 *Romola* had become the *Ladies Man* of 1931 and the glamorized and Hollywoodized Florenz Ziegfeld of 1936. The sinister Boldini of the 1926 *Beau Geste* was the tragic romantic of the 1932 *One Way Passage*. And when, in 1955, at age 63, Powell voluntarily retired, having gone out on top as "Doc" in *Mr. Roberts*, he had tallied, over 33 years, a host of varied characterizations that any actor might envy.

Through all of his personal vicissitudes, his career was his joy and consolation. Certainly his on-screen teaming with Myrna Loy in the *Thin Man* movies was a professional alliance made in Heaven. In my 1980 Citadel book, *The Films of Myrna Loy*, I quote her as telling an interviewer: "From the very first scene we did together in *Manhattan Melodrama* (1934), we felt that particular magic between us. There was this feeling of rhythm, of complete understanding, and an instinct of how each of us could bring out the best in the other."

The marriage of Powell's Nick and Loy's Nora was not based primarily on romantic sentiment, as in most movies of the time; rather it was grounded in the characters' realistic yet wryly affectionate, often amused awareness of each other's faults and foibles. Audiences found their mutual put-downs enthralling. Once, when Nora complained that she was in danger of becoming a widow, what with Nick's high-risk tailing of murderers, he countered with the tart observation that she wouldn't be a widow long—not with *her* money.

Enjoyment-oriented Nick lived off socialite Nora's money, and didn't care who knew it; retired from regular sleuthing, he kept bouncing back into it whenever an intriguing case turned up—which seemed to be often. Nora tagged along after Nick on his assorted adventures, deftly tennis-balling insult jokes; savoring martinis, Nick's favorite drink of the many drinks he consumed; standing mutually protective when the ice got thin; on hand in comradely togetherness for the obligatory wind-up with all the suspected murderers in one room waiting for exposure; and ending up happily contented in a domesticity of necessarily brief duration after a case well-solved, either with Asta, their wire-haired terrier (who in time was to become almost as big a hit with the fans as they were), or with the succession of babies-into-boys who portrayed Nick, Jr.

Along the way, in those thirteen pictures they did from 1934 to 1947, Loy became known cross-country as "The Perfect Wife," incidentally setting a new style in wives: She demonstrated that she could be Powell's companion and friend as well as bed-partner, could laugh along with him even when the laughs were turned on themselves, could be wry and gently, or not-so-gently, disapproving at times, but in the final analysis eminently supportive. In short, thanks to their cleverly written screenplays and wondrous mutual chemistry, they succeeded in convincing Americans of the 1930's and 1940's that marriage could be a barrel of laughs—and a lot of just plain fun.

As such they will always be remembered as the Screen's Perfect Marrieds. Although Powell had alternated between menacing and romancing the vivacious Bebe Daniels in their popular films of the 1920's, and although in the early 1930's he and Kay Francis had gone in for all-out romancing in the films they did together, in Loy, in 1934, Powell found the perfect complement on-screen. Their like has not been seen since. So "married" did they appear in picture after picture that fans refused to believe they weren't in real life; hence the myriad requests for marital advice from them that for years flooded the studios' mail rooms.

Though dogged throughout his life by personal tragedies—a first marriage that had gone sour, leaving him with a son who was for years a personal trial to him, and who finally committed suicide at age 43; a second marriage to Carole Lombard that had started off promisingly but fizzled within two years; a flaming mid-1930's romance with Jean

As a film villain, 1928.

Harlow that ended in shocking tragedy before he could marry her, and that left him emotionally shattered for years; and then a frightening and protracted bout with rectal cancer that, in 1938, when he was 46, had threatened to finish him once and for all—Powell kept his essential poise and inner composure, his philosophical spirit and fundamental balance. Completely devoid of self-pity, he remained resolutely positive, and endlessly patient.

At long last, the Law of Compensation asserted itself, and he found beautiful young MGM actress Diana Lewis, married her in 1940 when he was 47 and she was 21, and remained for 44 years her husband, finally dying—this man who had thought cancer would kill him at 46—at 91, in 1984.

A roller-coaster life, surely. But he survived everything, good and bad, sad and glad, into his tenth decade. That fundamental inner balance, the firm character, the level-headed, realistic approach to life, the sound inner schematic, all came to his aid. And because, all his life, Powell had been a disciplined planner and a dedicated worker who delighted in his craft and who had determined to make of his

great native talent a finely tuned instrument that would respond on command, he found that in many respects he was the captain of his fate and the master of his soul.

A cautious man free from major vices, Powell kept his long life free of scandal of any kind. His sex life between marriages was conducted with control and discretion—in romance, marriage and friendship alike, as well as in professional associations through a long career, he managed to emerge singularly liked, indeed admired.

He was to know many consolations along the way in addition to world fame—the sterling, lifetime male friendships with such fellow actors as Richard Barthelmess and Ronald Colman, the deep satisfaction in giving his aged parents a happy life in a house near his own in Hollywood. And always he was to be sustained by a mature philosophy, best expressed by such tenets of his as: "Happiness is a matter of inward disposition rather than outward circumstance" and "Cultivate solitude and quiet and a few sincere friends rather than mob merriment, noise, and thousands of nodding acquaintances."

Meticulous at all times, he rehearsed his roles carefully at home, was always letter-perfect in his reading when he reached the set—and later tended to go over his scripts and edit-out what he called "superfluous dialogue." "One or two gestures can be the equivalent of a whole page of some scripts," he said, "but those gestures have to have point and appropriateness."

The fundamental affirmation in his character seemed always to win the sympathy and trust of his audience, regardless of what side of the law his screen self found himself on; among his secrets for getting those people out there in the dark to love him were his urbane charm and lack of pretension, his civilized projection of inner humanity and humor. But he didn't lack a sense of humor about himself. Asked by one interviewer how he kept so slim and trim, he replied: "I highly recommend worrying. It is much more effective than dieting."

Powell has been described by more than one writer as a true gentleman. Yet he was far more than that. He was a man of considerable inner toughness and spiritual resilience, who over many years rode out passing storms of temporarily fading popularity, marital disasters, parental disillusion, and what appeared, at the time, frightening terminal illness. That superb toughness was forged in the hungry, chaotic years from 1912 to 1914, when, as a recent AADA graduate, he starved, suffered and struggled as a young actor in New York, sustained only by an adamant faith that an actor he was born to be, and an actor he would remain, do or die. This faith was forged in all the one-night stands and quick-playing weeks in stock and vaudeville, and weathered grimy hotel rooms and greasy-spoon diners in tank towns, the loneliness, the disappointments, the gumshoeing from one casting-office to another. There were plays that seemed initially so promising that closed out of New York, and plays that *did* open in New York, only to close a day or a week later.

But out of all that loneliness and despair and disappointment came the patience, the persistence, the determination to pry open that golden door of success, good fortune, the ultimate fulfillment of his talent. . . .

The beginning came on July 29, 1892, in Pittsburgh. An only child, he was the son of a public accountant, Horatio Warren Powell, and his wife, the former Nettie Brady. None of his family on either side had embraced show business, but his Irish mother was a merry soul who loved singing, dancing, and the theatrical troupes that passed through town. She recalled many years later that when she took the seven-year-old youngster to these theatricals, he would express keen interest, and would later do imitations of the players he had seen.

Circa 1901 Horatio Powell's work took him to Kansas City and banking tasks. A practical, unimaginative, and emotionally withdrawn man, he does not seem to have approved of his wife's and son's interest in matters theatrical, and sought to discourage it.

In high school in Kansas City, Powell took a renewed interest in theatricals. His father, determined to make a lawyer out of him, sent him to public speaking classes, since even at 17, in 1909, his resonant, well-pitched speaking voice had become apparent.

But the plan Horatio Powell had set in motion took an unexpected turn. Professor Dillenbeck, the public speaking teacher, took a shine to the boy's voice, helped him develop it, and one day urged him to try out for the Christmas play at the high school. He won the part, and was shortly playing Captain Absolute in Sheridan's *The Rivals.*

He won a favorable reaction from his audience, and began going to all the entertainments—plays, vaudeville, whatever—that played Kansas City. Meanwhile his father, at home, was pressing for him to enter law, and, anxious to please, Powell did attend the University of Kansas—for a few short weeks. Soon he was home, telling his disappointed parents that it was acting he really wanted, and that he wished to attend the American Academy of Dramatic Arts in New York.

An alarmed and disapproving Horatio Powell did his best to point out to his son the hazards of an actor's life, the financial insecurity, the lack of respect the profession suffered, the frequent unemployment "between engagements." He also gave it as his opinion that actors were immoral rogues who betrayed womanhood and led drunken, undisciplined lives. Powell countered with stories of successful actors who had won fame and fortune, such as Robert B. Mantell, James O'Neill, William Courtenay, John Drew. Horatio remained unimpressed. "A few swallows don't make a summer," he intoned, "and most swallows freeze in the winter cold."

Ignoring his father's admonitions, Powell went to work for the Kansas City Telephone Company, hoping to save enough from his small salary to go eventually to New York. Soon he realized it would take forever to accumulate enough. His father absolutely refused to subsidize him in New York, claiming that the money in the bank he had reserved for him would be used only for law studies.

Powell hit upon an idea. On his father's side, there was a wealthy aunt in Mercersburg, Pennsylvania. He wrote her a 24-page letter asking her for a loan of $1400 at six percent for two years, in order to finance his course at the American Academy of Dramatic Arts. In the letter, which he composed with utmost care born of total sincerity, he told of his acting dreams, of his conviction that it was the only vocation for him, the only thing he really wanted to do, the only thing for which, he felt, he had any true talent.

The letter worked. The aunt offered him half the amount—$700—and after figuring how he could make do on that, he quit his job and headed, despite his parents' loudly expressed misgivings, for New York and the Academy. He was not to repay the loan for a full decade. When he did, it was with full interest.

At the American Academy of Dramatic Arts he found himself in a class with such bright young hopefuls as Edward G. Robinson and Joseph Schildkraut. There he learned all the essential techniques. As a 1912 graduate, at age 20, he hunted jobs.

That 1912-1914 period he was to recall as the leanest, most frightening of his entire life. Too proud to ask for more money from home, (though his mother sent small sums when she could), he made endless rounds. He had met another young man named Ralph Barton, who was later to become a famous caricaturist for *Photoplay* and other national magazines— but that was in the future.

Powell and Barton took a room together, and proceeded to eat out of cans, pawn their clothes and watches when necessary, and cheer each other up with dreams of the future. Meanwhile Powell's alarmed father was begging him to come back to Kansas City and "go into something sensible." "You'll never have a home of your own, a wife, a child, any kind of permanence and security in that terrible life," he wrote, but Powell refused to go back. He knew there was nothing for him there.

For a while, it looked as though there would be nothing for him in New York, either, but then he got a small break—an offer of forty dollars a week to play three small bits in a play called *The Ne'er Do Well*, which debuted on

September 2, 1912, at Manhattan's Lyric Theatre. The play lasted only a few weeks.

After that came what Powell and Barton remembered later as "the toughest winter we ever spent in our lives." Barton remembers Powell at 21 as his classmates had recalled him at 17: "for the dramatic manner in which he recited entire chapters of the classics" and for "an almost visible mantle of aloofness which set him apart." Powell later claimed that his youthful "aloofness" was actually a cover-up for frightening insecurities.

Barton recalled that, at 21, Powell was no womanizer, and was not given to "dissipations" of any kind. "He was monk-like about his career; his career was everything to him." Barton also recalled that he felt Powell had a romanticized idea of women at the time, felt he should "save himself" for the right person. "He was a gentleman all right," Barton said. "The only expense he concerned himself with was decent clothes, essential for a burgeoning actor."

Powell haunted theatre lobbies on playing nights, eagerly surveying the billboards and looking wistfully at the richly dressed women and men who entered for the performance. When he could scare up a few cents, he got a high-balcony seat or standing room, where he studied the acting styles intently.

As 1913 wore on and his 21st birthday approached, Powell landed, through sheer persistence, jobs in vaudeville and stock playing out of town. It was in one of these stock companies that Powell first met up with the author's uncle, William P. Connery, Jr., then newly married and a struggling actor. My uncle, later to become a U.S. Congressman from Massachusetts, co-author of the Wagner-Connery Labor Relations Act and Chairman of the House Labor Committee in the Roosevelt Administration, had been an actor since 1909, struggling along in thankless stock company jobs all over the country. (This book is dedicated to him.)

After Powell became famous in the 1930's, my uncle, who had abandoned acting for politics after serving in the Army in France in World War I, used to regale us with stories of

In the Paramount commissary with Charles (Buddy) Rogers and Nancy Carroll.

their hardships in stock; he was to appear with Powell in various stock productions over the next three years, and he recalled that Powell was very dedicated to his work, very devoted to the young woman he married in 1914, at 22, hyper-serious, abstemious and hardworking. My uncle used to recall at family gatherings how Powell did his own laundry, keeping his collars white and stiff, and his clothes were personally pressed. He also concentrated completely on his role, even at that early age, and seemed to *become* the character he was playing. My uncle felt he did it through abstract intellectual concentration on the role, that he didn't do it emotionally or instinctively but through intellectual analysis.

My uncle also remembered that the young Powell had a roguish wit, a ready charm, and a sympathy for those around him who ran into bad luck; he added that he wasn't at all surprised when Powell made it big as a film star, because all that concentration and dedication had to pay off, given his already apparent talent.

Unpaid rehearsals, both on Broadway and in stock, were in that period the bane of the acting profession, and it was an abuse which was not to be corrected until after the Actors' Strike of 1919. My uncle and his wife, and Powell and *his* wife, were perpetually short of money; those grim, seedy hotel rooms, the bad food in sloppily run restaurants, the sparse, often rudely heckling audiences; he—and Powell—were later to remember the period as a nightmare that threatened never to end.

Powell met the girl he would later marry—Eileen Wilson—during one of those stock engagements. They were both playing in *Within the Law*, the road company of the Bayard Veiller drama, in which Powell, delighted to be rescued from absolute penury in New York, was to tour extensively in 1913-14. In the initial flush of young love, Powell and Eileen Wilson failed to realize that they were fundamentally incompatible. Powell's sense that marriage was stabilizing for him kept him from facing facts for a while, but eventually they split up.

There was not to be a divorce for many

Endorsing a *Photoplay Magazine* ad, 1931.

years—they even made up briefly in the mid-1920's, conceiving Powell's one child, William David, who was born in 1925. Later in the 1920's, asked by a reporter about his marriage, Powell was characteristically reticent, saying only, "Marriage does not seem to be for me; it's too much of an institution, and I like to come and go freely." Nonetheless, he felt guilt and a sense of failure over it, and worried about the effect of it upon his young son, whom he saw infrequently until he persuaded his mother to move them both, around 1930, to Hollywood.

But that was all yet ahead of the love-struck young newlyweds in 1914. One stock job followed on another. Eileen acted with him in many of them. They included the Harry Davis Stock Company in Pittsburgh, the Baker Company in Portland, Oregon, Jessie Bonstelle's in Buffalo. My uncle once tersely described stock company life as "exhilarating, in a crude way, but exasperating, and in a rough way," which said it all.

Powell in *Within the Law* had played a rather unpleasant character named English Eddie Griggs. "What I learned from English Eddie," Powell later said, "was that a villain can offer more range and excitement to an actor than a hero." Sometimes, in his anxiety to succeed, Powell got a little nervous in his performances, like a horse champing at the bit. One actress remembered him as "a long, lanky youth, all arms and legs. If there is anything onstage for him to trip over, he does. But he stands the company's teasing well."

In actuality, he was gaining in poise and authority—an authority some of his colleagues regarded as remarkable in a man 23 or so—as one role followed another in towns across the country. Finally, Powell hit Broadway again—in small parts in *The King* and *The Judge of Zalamea*. These plays starred a famous German-born actor and director named Leo Dietrichstein. Dietrichstein recognized the 24-year-old's talent at once, and schooled him in his technique. This was in 1916, and Dietrich-

16

stein's acting theories were just catching on. Powell had been schooled in the bravura, declamatory style of acting up to then; Dietrichstein taught him to look inside the character, to read between the lines. Bombast was to be eschewed at all times, and easy naturalism was to be the keynote.

A grateful Powell sopped up all the master had to tell him. Later he was to say of Dietrichstein: "He taught me all I know about acting."

After that Powell went from also-ran roles in briefly running Broadway plays to numerous out-of-town engagements. In 1917 he made it to Broadway once again in a musical comedy called *Going Up*, with the great Frank Craven, who, he later said, cued him in on numerous acting tricks and helped him to "nuance" and "pace" his characterizations. Donald Meek and Ruth Donnelly, later to be well-known film character actors, were also in the cast. The show was a hit and ran a record 351 performances. But Powell's role, a non-singing, non-dancing one, was small, and he made little impression.

Then it was back, circa 1919, to stock engagements at the Castle Square Company in Boston. This included Shakespearean plays, and Powell found Shakespeare, as well as other classic plays in the Castle Square repertory, a real challenge. "I grew as an actor playing Shakespeare," he later said. "That experience in Boston is one I will always be grateful for."

Three years of hard work in companies all over the nation followed, years of financial penury, years which witnessed the fading of his and Eileen Wilson's marriage. As his 30th birthday in 1922 approached, Powell found himself still struggling, still relatively unknown, with what little he earned going for his and his wife's lodgings, food and wardrobe.

Then came the turning point. It was a romantic melodrama called *Spanish Love*, and it opened on Broadway in 1922. It starred an old associate from the stock company days, James Rennie (later to be the husband of Dorothy Gish), and it gave Powell a role he could really get his teeth into—as a man who persists in his pursuit of love though he knows he is dying. The play was a hit, and the critics singled him out for special praise, with one calling him "the biggest sensation" in the show, and another commenting on his "touching emotional sensitivity and thrilling range."

Albert Parker, the film director, was in New York at the time and caught Powell's performance in *Spanish Love*. Later they met. "You would be a natural for movies," Parker told him. "You have an unusual face and a unique acting style, and you don't look like anyone else."

At 30, Powell realized that there was a premium on youth in the acting line, and that his hit in *Spanish Love* might well be followed by more thankless supporting roles in Broadway plays and leads in also-ran stock and vaudeville shows out of town. He decided to make a change. By 1922 the movies had become the booming entertainment industry. Possibly it might hold some chance of security and permanence for him.

When Parker offered him the part of Forman Wells, a villainous associate of the evil Professor Moriarity, in the John Barrymore *Sherlock Holmes*, Powell snapped at it. His role was small but tellingly delineated. He found films very different from the stage, much less demanding, with speech (in the silent period) irrelevant, and subtly modulated plays of facial expression the prevailing style. This he mastered easily.

It was back to the stage briefly, after this, and in the summer of 1922 he appeared on the stage for the last time, in a Broadway offering called *The Woman Who Laughed*. Then it was back to films, to the Cosmopolitan Studios in New York, where he played the comically villainous King Francis I in Marion Davies' *When Knighthood Was in Flower*. This was an elaborate 16th-century historical romance, with Davies' lover, William Randolph Hearst, sparing no expense in glamorizing her to the nines.

A bit player in *When Knighthood Was in Flower* was the author's father, Andrew L. Quirk, then a *Photoplay Magazine* staffer who took the assignment as a lark. Years later he

Gloria Swanson and Grace Moore sing a duet to the delight of Swanson's husband, Michael Farmer, and Powell at a party honoring Moore given by the Sidney Franklins, 1932.

recalled to me Powell's total concentration on his role, his meticulous preparation, his concern that every detail of his costume be accurate.

After this came a small role in an Elsie Ferguson film called *Outcast*. Then he went to Cuba to play a villain in the Richard Barthelmess-Dorothy Gish film *The Bright Shawl*, in which he played a heavy, a Spanish officer. During the making of this picture he formed a fast friendship with Richard Barthelmess, then a major silent star, who held Powell's talents in high regard. Later, in 1923, he worked in yet another costume movie, *Under the Red Robe*, in which he played another heavy. The Duc D'Orleans in *Under the Red Robe* offered him some characterizational range, and he did not go unnoticed by some of the critics, one of whom referred to him as "that unusual-looking actor with the prominent eyes and distinctive bearing."

Editor James R. Quirk of *Photoplay*, who had seen Powell on the stage and had taken note of his screen progress, wrote that Powell was "a distinctive actor with a seasoned style who deserves more prominent casting—and coverage—than he has so far received." Quirk boosted Powell whenever he could, and, as in the case of another of his favorite actors, Fredric March, touted Powell with producers. Eventually a long-term contract with Paramount was to be the result.

But that contract was a year or two away when Powell appeared for the first time with Bebe Daniels in a film called *Dangerous Money*. It was to be the first of a number of pictures he and the vivacious, sparkling-eyed Daniels would make together during the middle and late 1920's—in some he was the villain giving her a hard time (as he was in *Dangerous Money*); in others he would be romancing her, after a fashion, but the public seemed to like them together.

Another 1924 release was the much-publicized *Romola*, which starred Lillian and Dorothy Gish, with Powell as Tito Melema, a Renaissance Italian villain who made the Gish girls mighty unhappy before the fadeout. The film also had Ronald Colman in the cast, and another lifetime friendship was born between him and Powell.

Like Powell, Colman had endured a bad marriage, and considered what Powell called "an institution" to be a pernicious trap. Later, he, Powell and Barthelmess were to be the merriest bachelor threesome offscreen, until all finally remarried. For years they were known as The Three Musketeers.

Romola was considered a stately, dignified bore when it finally appeared, but it was the film that was to be instrumental in winning Powell his Paramount contract, as he appeared to considerable advantage in it, having the central role. James R. Quirk told Adolph Zukor of Paramount: "You can't ignore this man any more; you've got to have him in your stable!"

During *Romola*'s shooting in Italy, in the summer of 1924, Powell went to Venice for a romantic vacation, and there, by accident, met his by-now-estranged wife, Eileen Wilson. Caught up in the exotic ambience, they got

18

Mervyn LeRoy rehearsing Powell, Evelyn Brent and other cast members for *High Pressure* (1932.)

together again briefly, conceiving his only child, William David, born the next year. But there was to be no enduring reconciliation for them, and soon Powell was back bacheloring it with Colman and Barthelmess, while conducting discreet liaisons with willing ladies.

In the Paramount pictures that followed, pictures with titles like *Too Many Kisses, Faint Perfume, My Lady's Lips,* and *Aloma of the South Seas,* Powell tended to villainize more than he romanced. But his vivid face and expressions and poised bearing and aplomb made him a popular player, sought after by directors. Secure now in a long-term Paramount contract, he concentrated on his specialty: stealing the picture from the nominal "hero."

The roles varied little. In *Partners in Crime* he was a bad boy indeed. In *The Runaway,* a backstage story, he romanced Clara Bow, the "It" girl. In *Aloma of the South Seas* he was a heavy who watched Gilda Gray shimmy. In *Desert Gold* he was a Western bad man.

Director John Cromwell, crouched with pipe at lower right, guides Ann Harding and Powell during making of *Double Harness,* 1933. The crew looks on.

19

Director Woody Van Dyke clowns with Powell and Loy on set of *The Thin Man,* 1934. Henry Wadsworth, left, and Maureen O'Sullivan, between Van Dyke and Powell, join in the fun.

Powell and Edward G. Robinson visit Dolores Del Rio and Ricardo Cortez during a dance rehearsal for *Wonder Bar,* 1933.

Powell and Loy during a 1934 radio broadcast.

Powell and his second wife, Carole Lombard, at a costume party.

In 1926 he got a chance to give two telling characterizations—as an unlettered garage man who kills Gatsby (Warner Baxter) in the film version of F. Scott Fitzgerald's *The Great Gatsby,* and as an oily thief, Boldini, who tries to steal a jewel from Ronald Colman in *Beau Geste* and dies in a spectacular suicide.

After playing foil to his perennial vis-à-vis Bebe Daniels in such films as *She's a Sheik* (he was an Arab brigand) and *Senorita* (again he was her nemesis), Powell got his best break yet, as the director, a former revolutionist, who humiliates former Tsarist Russian general Emil Jannings on a movie set in Josef Von Sternberg's *The Last Command.* By this time Powell was permanently settled in Hollywood, where he was much sought after by the social elite, to say nothing of every unattached lady in town. Being normally sexed, he conducted discreet affairs, but handled them with such gallantry and tact that not a woman in Hollywood could be found to say one unkind word about him.

The Last Command, released early in 1928,

Friends Powell, center, Ronald Colman, left, and Richard Barthelmess, right, go yachting, circa 1931.

With his great and good friend, Richard Barthelmess.

earned Powell some fine notices. It was a prestige production, meticulously directed by Von Sternberg, and Powell felt it was a plus to appear with the great Jannings, who was to win an Oscar for his performance in this. The biting realism and the consummate ironies in the screenplay and performances were much admired, and Powell, who had felt he was languishing unduly in the pedestrian fare Paramount accorded him, now felt he had made some major advances with this well-received film.

After some more creditable performances in essentially lacklustre films— such as *Beau Sabreur* (he was a heavy), *Feel My Pulse* (again with Daniels), *Forgotten Faces* and *The Vanishing Pioneer* (he was a menace in both), Powell found that his luck had changed via the new talkie boom and his appearance in Paramount's first full-fledged talkie, *Interference*.

For the first time, the fans heard his voice, and his stock went up tremendously. Audiences across the country received the *talking* William Powell ecstatically, with Elinor Hughes in *The Boston Herald* writing: "His cultivated and expressive voice, his smooth, polished manner and easy assumption of emotion masked under flippant cynicism made him the outstanding actor in a cast that included Clive Brook, Evelyn Brent and Doris Kenyon."

Paramount thereupon decided that William Powell, the also-ran supporting player in so many of their 1925-1928 films, the shunted-aside menace and hissed villain who had only occasionally been allowed to romance the heroine, was worthy of the star build-up. They next cast him in *The Canary Murder Case,* made first as a silent and then as a talkie. In his first appearance as Philo Vance, smooth, dapper, silky and aristocratic, with a knack for spotting murderers, Powell won even more fans. During 1929 and 1930 he was seen in two more Philo Vance efforts, (*The Greene Murder Case* and *The Benson Murder Case*), both successful. He then expertly played Ruth Chatterton's lover (Clive Brook was her errant husband) in *Charming Sinners* (the film version of Ethel Barrymore's 1926 Broadway hit, *The Constant Wife*), and became a popular star in *Street of Chance* (a gambler), *Shadow of the Law* (an innocent man sent to prison), and *For the Defense* (an attorney who bribes a juror).

Powell was now getting many bags of fan mail. He was riding the crest of the popularity wave, and at this point decided on two courses of action in his personal life. At 38, he had been living, off and on, with such bachelor friends as Richard Barthelmess, and felt he needed more settled conditions. He brought his father and mother to Hollywood and made his father his business manager. This way he was enabled to keep an eye on them in their declining years and assure that they had every comfort his large salary from Paramount now made possible. He then asked his estranged wife to bring herself and his son to live in Hollywood; agreeing with him that their five-year-old boy needed a father's concern as well as a mother's, Eileen settled herself and the child in a nearby house, where he was free to visit young William frequently. Relations between Powell and his ex-wife were cooperative and amiable, his usual style in all his personal dealings.

In 1931, Powell was seen in two aptly-titled films, *Man of the World,* in which he was a charming blackmailer and ladies' nemesis in Paris, and *Ladies' Man,* in which he was a charming cad who lived off women until murdered by an irate husband.

During this period he did a number of films with the lovely Kay Francis, who proceeded to have an affair with him offscreen that lasted a season or two. In such pictures as *Street of Chance, For the Defense, Ladies' Man* and, later at Warners in 1932, in such items as *Jewel Robbery* and the famous *One Way Passage,* the Powell-Francis combination made quite an impression on the fans, and reached a peak of popularity that was to be exceeded only by the Loy-Powell teaming of 1934. Their chemistries—on screen and, for a time, offscreen—were mutually right, and the fans sensed the emotional current between Powell and Francis—for a time.

By 1931 the Francis affair was cooling down, and Powell met and fell in love, during

Director Victor Fleming, Powell and Jean Harlow during *Reckless* filming, 1935.

On a date with Jean Harlow at the Hollywood Bowl, 1935.

With his son, William Powell, Jr. about 1936.

As Jetta Goudal pouts, Powell and another officer exchange glares. *(The Bright Shawl)*

and enmities with the Spanish military, chief among them Powell, who plays Gaspar de Vaca, a Spanish officer who is up to no good. Barthelmess falls in love with Mary Astor, sister of his Cuban friend, Andre Beranger.

Dorothy Gish is on hand as Lᵃ Clavel, an Andalusian dancer (it was her second film with Powell) who falls in love with Barthelmess and feeds him information that she pries from the Spanish. Jetta Goudal is a Spanish spy who traps Beranger's family, with Gish giving her life for Barthelmess. Later Barthelmess, Astor and her mother (Margaret Seddon) manage to escape back to the United States.

Edward G. Robinson was also prominently spotted, in this his first picture; fresh from a fine stage career, he was billed as E.G. Robinson, and played Domingo Escobar, a Cuban patriot. Powell as chief villain has some strong

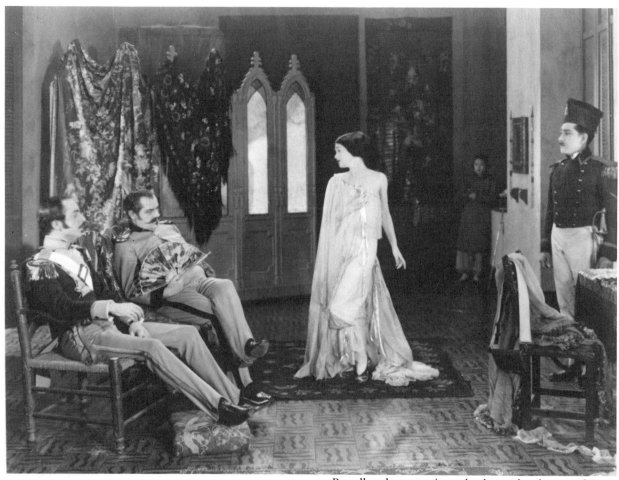

Powell and companions check out the charms of Jetta Goudal. *(The Bright Shawl)*

As a gag, Powell and Loy show up wearing clown's shoes for placing in cement at Grauman's Chinese Theatre. That's Sid Grauman with them.

Alice Brady and Powell relax with a game of monopoly on set of *My Man Godfrey*, 1936.

the shooting of *Man of the World,* with a vital young actress on the way up, Carole Lombard. They appeared in another 1931 film, *Ladies' Man,* made an instant decision to marry, and on June 26, 1931, did so.

The marriage was doomed from the start. Lombard at 22 had not matured sufficiently for the constrictions of marriage, or for the inherent responsibilities, and Powell at 39, who had finally asked Eileen for a divorce to marry Lombard, discovered that he had not sloughed off his bachelor ways, and was once more forced to regard marriage, even to the vivacious Lombard, as a constricting "institution."

Also, their temperaments were too different. Lombard liked to be out on the town; Powell was a retiring soul. Lombard was instinctual; Powell was cerebral. Lombard admitted later that she had learned a lot from Powell about acting and about the life of intellect and culture, and he always spoke of her with warm affection and understanding, but by 1933 they had parted, with a divorce following. By 1934 they were astonishing Hollywood by dating frequently, and Powell continued to give Lombard advice on her career and personal problems. "We made better friends than we did as marrieds," Lombard told a 1933 interviewer, "and now, free of marriage, we can enjoy the friendship fully, without ties or obligations."

Powell said of Lombard, "She was ready to spread her wings, and marriage enabled her to do it."

Powell was always on the lookout for better opportunities, as he was determined to make "The William Powell Acting Business," as he and his parents dubbed it, a continuing major success. When his Paramount contract expired, he went with Warners for more money. He was with them for only two years, during which he made his hits with Kay Francis, and such items as *Lawyer Man* and *Private Detective 62* (the titles speak for themselves), another Philo Vance movie, *The Kennel Murder Case* (Warners hoped to cash in on Powell's success in the earlier Vance films at Paramount), *Fashions of 1934* with Bette Davis (they mixed like

the proverbial oil and water in what fans and critics found an amusing clash of styles and chemistries), and *The Key,* in which Powell played a British officer dallying with another officer's wife during the Irish uprising of 1922.

By early 1934, with his latest Warner films doing indifferent business, the word was getting around that Powell was "washed up." Warners, caught at the bottom of the Depression and suffering financial strictures, did not want to pay his large salary. Powell took these ominous events in stride, and, with his usual philosophical reaction, promptly got himself a top agent and went over to Metro-Goldwyn-Mayer—at first on a tentative deal.

Louis B. Mayer and other studio executives in early 1934 tended to go along with the general opinion in Hollywood that Powell was on the way out, but the brilliant performance he gave in *Manhattan Melodrama* with Clark Gable and Myrna Loy, and the fine boxoffice returns, promptly changed their minds.

Then director W. S. (Woody) Van Dyke talked Mayer into letting him use Powell and Myrna Loy together in *The Thin Man*—and it was a smash, earning two million dollars on a

Signing autographs during a reception at Maxim's, Paris, 1937.

25

On the town with Connie Bennett and Gilbert Roland, Powell congratulates ice skating speed champions at a sports event, circa 1935.

With Marlene Dietrich, Loretta Young and George Cukor at the Trocadero, 1940.

With Arthur Hornblow Jr., Diana Lewis, his third wife, and Myrna Loy, 1940.

nominal investment and a 14-day shooting schedule.

Only six months after he had been called "washed up," William Powell was on top of the Hollywood heap again. The characters of Nick and Nora, as limned by Powell and Loy, were portrayed as the fans had never seen married people portrayed; their larkish adventures as they solved murders and their affectionate badinage with each other enthralled audiences all over the country.

Knowing a good thing when they saw it, MGM promptly cast Powell and Loy again, in *Evelyn Prentice,* in which he was a lawyer and she his wife who gets involved with a blackmailer. After a loan-out stint at RKO in *Star of Midnight* (1935) (in the 1933-1936 period he was to be loaned to RKO for several films, including the drawing room drama, *Double Harness,* with Ann Harding in 1933, and the *Thin Man*-style reprise, *The Ex-Mrs. Bradford,* with Jean Arthur in 1936), Powell went on to *Reckless,* during which his burgeoning friendship with Jean Harlow ripened into love. Meanwhile Powell won his first Academy Award nomination for *The Thin Man,* and went on to *Escapade* (1935) a picture about romantic intrigue in Vienna which he practi-

With his third wife, Diana Lewis, 1940.

27

cally handed to the newcomer from Austria, Luise Rainer, showing his generous and helpful spirit by making sure the camera angles and direction favored her so as to show her to initial advantage with the fans. She was always to be grateful to Powell for that.

He did pretty much the same thing for another new actress, Rosalind Russell, in the spy story that followed, *Rendezvous*. Both the Rainer and Russell parts had been intended for Myrna Loy (the fans were clamoring for more Powell-Loy films) but Loy, feeling she was not being paid enough money, went on a strike of sorts until she got what she felt was due her, given her fast rise on the popularity polls.

The year 1936 was to see Powell at his zenith. Four of his five released movies that year were smash hits. At the request of Billie Burke, widow of Florenz Ziegfeld, he played the showman in *The Great Ziegfeld* to great acclaim. A lavish three-hour affair, it showcased him with Rainer again, and also with Myrna Loy, who had returned to the studio under terms she felt more favorable. *My Man Godfrey*, made on loan to Universal, teamed him yet again with his ex-wife and cordial continuing friend, Carole Lombard, in the greatest of the screwball comedies. He was reunited with his current love, Jean Harlow, Loy and Spencer Tracy in *Libeled Lady*, another smash hit; and rounded out 1936 with a second *Thin Man* picture, *After The Thin Man*, with Loy.

Powell went into the year 1937 with all colors flying. His chemistry and Joan Crawford's, however, did not blend well in the second film version of Frederick Lonsdale's *The Last of Mrs. Cheyney* (Crawford and Bette Davis were never to be right for Powell, onscreen anyway), but Powell, reunited with Luise Rainer in the baroque European spy romance, *The Emperor's Candlestick*, was hailed as his usual charming and charismatic self; and *Double Wedding,* released later in 1937, reteamed him delightfully with Loy.

Then Powell's luck changed. A tragedy and a near-tragedy were to assail him in 1937-1938. Jean Harlow died suddenly of uremic poisoning on June 7, 1937; in increasingly bad health, beset by her mother's peculiar ideas about Christian Science "healing," Harlow had pushed herself to finish a picture called *Saratoga* with Clark Gable. She died three quarters of the way through the shooting, and a double finished the film. Powell was thrown into deep shock by her death, and appeared in tears at the funeral.

He had been hesitant about marriage with Harlow, much as he loved her; she, on the other hand, had been desperate to marry him, and he felt guilty that he had not honored her wish. But she had already had three failed marriages, and he had had two, and he did not feel that either of them were suited to the married state. Harlow, unnerved by the suicide of her second husband, MGM producer Paul Bern, in 1932, only two months after her marriage to him, resentful at Louis B. Mayer for having cast her, in her first picture with Powell, *Reckless*, in a role that recalled the suicide, and the mysterious death of Libby Holman's young husband, Zachary Reynolds, the same year as Bern's death, felt besieged from all sides, and hoped to find a safe emotional harbor in Powell. But it was not to be.

Racked with remorse and a guilt that his friends found excessive, Powell purchased an expensive crypt at Forest Lawn Cemetery, with room for three bodies, reportedly hers, her mother's—and his. His sympathetic friend Ronald Colman made his yacht available to him while he recovered from Harlow's death, and then, wishing to avoid all reminders of her, he went to Europe, where he shot location scenes, in late 1937, in Hungary for *The Baroness and the Butler*, with Annabella. In 1936 and 1937 Powell was named one of the top box office stars, and his salary estimates for each year ran between $400,000 and $650,000. He also won a second Oscar nomination in 1936 for *My Man Godfrey*.

Then the second of the crises hit Powell. A painful and embarrassing rectal examination revealed that he had cancer. Determined to lick the odds, Powell underwent an operation in early 1938 that involved a temporary colostomy and severely weakened his condition.

Taking instruction from director Richard Thorpe on the set of *The Thin Man Goes Home*, 1944.

With Howard Lindsay, co-author and star of the stage version of *Life With Father*, and Irene Dunne on the set of the film version, 1947.

His chances of surviving, at first, were thought not to be good. During most of 1938 he did nothing but rest, and made no further films. The studio covered up his true physical condition and let it be known that "stomach ulcers" were the cause.

In late 1938, with his strength slowly returning, Powell did some radio work. In early 1939, with his cancer obviously in what turned out to be permanent remission, he submitted to a second operation that reversed the colostomy and sent his elimination system back to normal—but at the cost of considerable energy. For months he rested at home.

At last, in the fall of 1939, Powell returned to MGM for *Another Thin Man*. Myrna Loy, director Woody Van Dyke and the other members of the company put him on a 10 a.m. to 4 p.m. shooting schedule, and did everything to speed up the production with a view to making it easy for him. He completed the picture successfully.

Then Powell's life brightened again, with a wonderful new renaissance occurring in his personal life. In 1939, at age 47, he met fledgling MGM actress Diana Lewis, then 21. After knowing each other only six weeks, they were married in January, 1940. Powell's friends at first felt he had been too hasty, and that the alliance would not last. But it turned out to be a surprising success—and continued until Powell's death, 44 years later.

A sensible, level-headed young woman, Lewis had been in vaudeville in childhood, when she trouped with her parents. She had gone on from that to chorus work and nightclub singing and then into films. Free of a compulsive career drive, seeking only to assure her new husband's happiness and comfort, Diana Lewis turned into the greatest life-blessing Powell was ever to receive. She even got on well with his troubled 14-year-old son, William David, who as he reached teen years began to show signs of increasing emotional instability, failing to adjust to a series of expensive schools and otherwise proving irritatingly recalcitrant.

Happy in his marriage, Powell made but one film in 1940, *I Love You Again*, with Loy,

then in 1941 did two more with her, the hilarious *Love Crazy* and *Shadow of the Thin Man*. As his health slowly improved, he went on to *Crossroads,* and *The Heavenly Body,* both with Hedy Lamarr, then, after a cameo stint in a movie about fanatical autograph hunters, *The Youngest Profession* (1943), did his fifth *Thin Man* picture with Myrna Loy, *The Thin Man Goes Home.*

By 1945, Powell, then 53, was definitely slipping at the box office, and he was delighted to note, he told a reporter, that it didn't particularly bother him. "I had a good long run, better than many people's in my racket. I'd like to do a few more good films, but I'm philosophical," he said, "I have a lovely wife and my health, and for that I am profoundly grateful."

Nevertheless he grew increasingly impatient with the nothing roles that MGM was handing him. He appeared in two for them in the year 1946—*Ziegfeld Follies,* in which he was, for a brief moment or two at the beginning, Florenz Ziegfeld looking down from Heaven at an edition of The Follies, and *The Hoodlum Saint,* in which he "could have phoned in his performance" as one critic put it, as an ambitious financier who gets hooked on St. Dismas, The Good Thief, after he is hit by financial reverses in the 1929 crash. Critics shook their collective heads over what one called "a waste of Mr. Powell's superior talents."

MGM's only bright idea for Powell in 1947 was one more, last-gasp retread of the *Thin Man* formula. Again co-starred with Loy in what most reviewers agreed was a tired, thin, outdated confection, Powell looked worn and much too old for Nick Charles. He was by then 55 years old.

But there was to be a Last Hurrah for William Powell. For five years he had begged Louis B. Mayer to purchase the hit Broadway play *Life With Father* for him. He had known instinctively that the benign 1880's patriarchal curmudgeon Clarence Day was right for him, that it would give him a chance to re-demonstrate, to critics and fans, his wide characterizational range. Mayer had demurred on his request, feeling the asking price for screen rights—$500,000—was too steep.

To Powell's profound delight, Jack Warner, one of his earlier bosses who had always liked and admired him, purchased the play and invited him to come on loan to Warners to play Clarence Day opposite Irene Dunne. Mayer acceded to the loanout, and Powell proceeded with the role of his career.

The picture, when released in late 1947, was a signal success, and put Powell back on top again. Howard Barnes of *The New York Herald-Tribune* wrote, "[Powell] gave the greatest performance of a highly distinguished career, altogether the best of the mummers who have donned a red wig to celebrate a curious patriarchy." Alton Cook in *The New York World-Telegram and Sun,* enthused, "He has summoned up a robust gusto that no other role ever indicated was among his resources," and *The New York Times* reviewer opined, "Even his voice, always so distinctive, has taken on a new quality, so completely has Mr. Powell managed to submerge his own personality. His Father is not merely a performance; it is a character delineation of a high order, and he so utterly dominates the picture that even when he is not on hand his presence is still felt."

For *Life With Father,* Powell garnered his third Academy Award nomination, but was to lose to his old friend *Ronald Colman,* whose *A Double Life* was the sensation of the year. Powell, however, consoled himself with the highly prestigious New York Film Critics award.

After *Life With Father,* Powell went on loan to Universal-International for *The Senator Was Indiscreet,* a Washington satire about an old political mountebank, of which Cecelia Ager in *PM* wrote "His characterization is a beauty, worthy of . . . everyone's rousing cheers." Another critic enthused: "Mr. Powell is shifting into characterizations of late that do away with the personality that made him so popular and instead display him as an actor of wide range and infinite resource—a consummation devoutly to be wished."

His next two for Universal-International,

With Hedda Hopper on the set of *The Senator Was Indiscreet,* 1947.

Take One False Step (he's a professor suspected of murder) and *Mr. Peabody and the Mermaid* (he's a stuffy Bostonian who—you guessed it—romances that fish-tail girl), were only mild successes, and the odd film he did at 20th Century-Fox, *Dancing in the Dark,* a semi-musical in which he was a faded star who helps his child, whom he doesn't know is his, become a musical success, failed to register decisively.

Happy in his domestic life, and fulfilled by having done what he called "the all-time role of my career" (*Life With Father*), Powell at 58 was inclined to take things easy, and, except for a small and forgettable role in an all-star film for MGM, *It's a Big Country,* was not seen on the screen for some three years.

When he returned in a confused Universal programmer, *Treasure of Lost Canyon,* in 1952, it was by no means a fitting celebration for his approaching sixtieth birthday. The picture ended up on the second half of double bills.

The next year, 1953, found him, at age 61, on display in his final Metro-Goldwyn-Mayer picture, *The Girl Who Had Everything,* a remake of the Norma Shearer-Clark Gable-Lionel Barrymore hit of 1931, based on a story by

With Cary Grant at lunch, circa 1948.

Adela Rogers St. Johns. Powell got a chance to shine as the criminal lawyer who tries to save his daughter from a romance with an outlaw type. The young Elizabeth Taylor, who had first appeared with Powell in *Life With Father*, played his daughter here, and he was billed third after her and Fernando Lamas as the criminal whose dalliance with Taylor Powell resents.

Next it was over to 20th Century-Fox for *How to Marry a Millionaire*, in which this veteran of numerous pairings on screen with the top leading ladies of four filmic decades got to sample the likes of Lauren Bacall, Betty Grable—and Marilyn Monroe.

In this concoction about three ambitious girls out to snag rich husbands, Powell was the millionaire who becomes involved with Lauren Bacall until she chooses the younger Cameron Mitchell, a rich boy pretending for a time to be poor in order to test her love. A

number of the reviewers of *How to Marry a Millionaire* opined that Powell's mature and depthful, as well as feyly-comical, performance held the whole thing up.

For his last picture, two years later at Warners, Powell appeared as the world weary, understanding, but on occasion roguishly scampish "Doc" in the cinematization of the stage hit *Mr. Roberts*. Surrounded by powerhouse co-stars Henry Fonda, James Cagney and Jack Lemmon, Powell more than held his own. "The role of Doc is more self-effacing and quietly conceived than the others," one New York critic maintained, "but in the expert hands of William Powell, it comes alive and burns with its own highly distinctive glow."

With *Mr. Roberts* under his belt, Powell decided, at age 63, that the time had come for all-out retirement. He had all the money he would ever need, having invested wisely during his years of large earnings, and moreover he was eligible for the MGM pension plan for all his years of service there; even though he didn't need the pension, it was still nice to have it, for the principle of the thing, he confided to one reporter.

The television people tried to lure him back to co-star with Myrna Loy, but much as he loved Myrna, he felt his time had come to bow out of all media and settle into his private life in Palm Springs with Diana, his beloved "Mousie." Melvyn Douglas was assigned to the TV role opposite Loy.

Only one tragic incident was to disturb the nearly 30 years of domestic tranquillity that Powell and Lewis would enjoy in Palm Springs. On March 13, 1968, the Los Angeles police telephoned the 75-year-old Powell with the sad news that his only child, William David Powell, age 43, had stabbed himself to death. He had left a note for Powell which was not divulged, except a statement to the effect that

he hoped to go to a better world than he had found here.

The younger Powell had had an erratic, unhappy career. Married twice and divorced twice, he had graduated from Princeton, a college his father had always wished to attend and had wistfully visited while in a stock company nearby in the long-ago. Then he had gone into the Marines. Later he had served in the Korean War.

After working as a television writer and producer, his health had failed, and he found himself besieged with hepatitis and kidney trouble that proved permanent, and in time prevented him from working. It had all gotten to be too much for him, and he had ended his life. His mother, Eileen Wilson, had died in 1942.

Powell reportedly was sunk in grief for several years.

As the years went on, "Mousie" busied her-

With Marilyn Monroe at the Racquet Club, Palm Springs, 1954.

self with a painting hobby and with sports. Powell swam regularly in the private pool attached to their Palm Springs house and enjoyed giving dinner parties for Lewis's friends from the surrounding area. A talented artist, Lewis became a founding member of the Palette Club of California, a club for burgeoning painters which sponsored scholarships and art courses. Mrs. Powell enjoyed bowling, tennis and golf, and sponsored the "Mousetrap Open," a golf tournament for amateurs and other enthusiasts.

As he approached his 90th year, Powell found himself besieged with diabetes and was forced to take insulin shots every day. Then he grew deaf, and his eyes started to go. He was cheered by visits from old friends like Myrna Loy, who made it a point to journey to Palm Springs every time she came to Hollywood from her permanent base in New York.

The man who had said at 33 that marriage was an "institution" in which he felt trapped and constricted, found that his wife of over 40 years was the great staff and comfort of his life as he passed 90 and his life neared its end. She was all he had, as his parents had passed on decades before, along with his son, and most of his old friends, like Richard Barthelmess and Ronald Colman, had also long since died.

In the year before he died, Diana Lewis Powell told a friend, "I love him more now than the day I married him," and Powell responded with, "I'd have been a dead man without her. She's my life."

A friend remembers visiting the Powells in the last months of his life. "I was shocked by his appearance. He was white-haired and shriveled. But Diana bubbled around him, and was affectionate with him and joked with him."

Diana Lewis Powell, by then herself 65, recalled later that in the week before he passed on, Powell had been alert and in good spirits. The end came suddenly, on Monday, March 5, 1984. William Powell would have been 92 on the following July 29.

It was left to Myrna Loy, by then 78 and in poor health in her home in New York, to give the most fitting eulogy for her old friend. In her statement to the press, she said, "I never enjoyed my work more than when I worked with William Powell. He was a brilliant actor, a delightful companion, a great friend, and above all, a true gentleman."

Original art work of Powell and Loy as Nick and Nora, by Bob Harman

Powell in his first film role, sans moustache, as the scoundrelly henchman of Holmes's arch-enemy, Professor Moriarty. *(Sherlock Holmes)*

SHERLOCK HOLMES

1922 GOLDWYN PICTURES

CAST:

John Barrymore *(Sherlock Holmes);* Roland Young *(Dr. Watson);* Carol Dempster *(Alice Faulkner);* Gustav von Seyffertitz *(Professor Moriarty);* William H. Powell *(Forman Wells);* Louis Wolheim *(Craigin);* Percy Knight *(Sid Jones);* Hedda Hopper *(Madge Larrabee);* Anders Randolf *(James Larrabee);* Peggy Bayfield *(Rose Faulkner);* Margaret Kemp *(Therese);* Reginald Denny *(Prince Alexis);* David Torrence *(Count Van Stalburg);* Lumsden Hare *(Dr. Leighton).*

CREDITS:

Albert Parker (Director); F.J. Godsol (Producer); Marion Fairfax, Earle Browne (Scenario); based on the Sherlock Holmes tales of Conan Doyle; J. Roy Hunt (Photographer). Also derived from the William Gillette play.

Running time, 9 reels. Released May, 1922.

ESSAY

Photoplay Magazine, the screen's leading journal in the 1920's, had glowing praise for the John Barrymore version of *Sherlock Holmes* in its July 1922 issue. Of this first of William Powell's 95 movies, *Photoplay* wrote: "It is one of the most artistic and unusual films ever made. Its settings and photography are amazingly fine. Its cast is one of the few real all-star affairs."

Powell, who was delighted and honored to be supporting an actor he idolized, John Barrymore, plays a rather unpleasant character named Forman Wells, and the hooded eyes and ill-disguised sneer on his face—without moustache—got across, in the accompanying picture, the malevolence of his brief and not-too-well-defined role, as he sought to foil, along with other miscreants, Barrymore's efforts to find a thieving culprit. For this and a few subsequent films, Powell billed himself as William *H.* Powell (middle initials were a fashion for stage actors in the first two or three decades of this century, a holdover from the nineteenth century).

As a scheming aide of Professor Moriarty (Gustav Von Seyffertitz), Holmes's arch-enemy, Powell made a good impression in his all-too-brief but telling appearance. He was to recall in later years that acting in movies seemed easier than on the stage, because there was no dialogue to learn and it was all done with appropriate expressions and graceful, but planned, movements that had to be kept within camera range at all times. He did recall that his first film director, Albert Parker, had to warn him about the marks that kept him properly placed before the cameras, and about the necessity of scaling-down his expressions as the camera picked up the smallest flickers of facial nuance.

Barrymore he found pleasant and charming. The great actor was only one of many who played Holmes over the years, including Clive Brook and, above all, Basil Rathbone, who took a patent on the role later. The plot here had to do with a Prince (Reginald Denny) who with Holmes's help is cleared of a theft charge. Roland Young was a delightful Dr. Watson in a role that Nigel Bruce later made his very own, and Carol Dempster was Barrymore-Holmes's love interest.

WHEN KNIGHTHOOD WAS IN FLOWER

1922 COSMOPOLITAN–PARAMOUNT

CAST:

Marion Davies *(Princess Mary Tudor);* Forrest Stanley *(Charles Brandon);* Lyn Harding *(King Henry VIII);* Theresa Maxwell Conover *(Queen Catherine);* Pedro De Cordoba *(Duke of Buckingham);* William Norris *(King Louis XII of France);* William H. Powell *(King Francis I of France);* Ruth Shepley *(Lady Jane Bolingbroke);* Ernest Glendenning *(Sir Edwin Caskoden);* Arthur Forrest *(Cardinal Wolsey);* Downing Clarke *(Lord Chamberlain);* Gustav von Seyffertitz *(Gramont);* Paul Panzer *(Captain of the Guard);* Guy

The wedding of Davies to the aging Louis XII of France (William Norris). Powell is second from right in first row, with Forrest Stanley on his right. Andrew Quirk, father of the author, is in moustache behind the officiating archbishop's mitre, third from left. *(When Knighthood Was in Flower)*

Powell as the new king menaces Davies, whom he seeks to possess. *(When Knighthood Was in Flower)*

37

Coombes *(Follower of Buckingham);* Andrew Quirk *(Courtier).*

CREDITS:

Robert G. Vignola (Director); Luther Reed (Screenplay and Adaptation from the novel); Ira Morgan, Harold Wenstrom (Photographers); Joseph Urban (Set Designer); William Frederick Peters (Music); Philip Carle (Assistant Director).

Running time, 12 reels. Released September, 1922.

ESSAY

Powell's Shakespearean training on the stage stood him in good stead when he took over from another actor (who had been in an accident) the part of Francis I, King of France, in a lavish costume epic called *When Knighthood Was in Flower.* This was produced by William Randolph Hearst's Cosmopolitan Productions and starred his mistress, Marion Davies. No expense was stinted on it, and Joseph Urban's settings and Robert G. Vignola's direction of a romantic drama, based on a Charles Major 1898 book, exceeded all Hearst's expectations of a top-quality mounting for his beloved Marion, whose true talents were in comedy but whom Hearst loved to keep in lavish costume films.

My father, Andrew Quirk, then a newlywed and *Photoplay Magazine* staffer, got a role as a bit player in the court scenes, courtesy of his brother James Quirk's friendship with Hearst and Robert Vignola, and he recalled to me years later the atmosphere of relaxed camaraderie on the set, due to Davies's unassuming kindness to all about her. He remembered Powell (still billed as William *H.*) concentrating intensely on his role. My father can be seen in the background of one of the accompanying stills, as noted in the caption.

The story had Davies, as Mary Tudor, sister of King Henry VIII (Lyn Harding,) in love with a commoner (Forrest Stanley), but who is forced to marry, for reasons of state, the aging King Louis XII of France (William Norris). Davies extracts a condition, that upon the king's death, if she survives, she can choose her next husband. Shortly after the nuptials,

Louis XII dies, and his successor, Francis I (Powell) tries to take her over, but Davies resists him and eventually manages, after some vicissitudes, to marry her original true love.

Sporting a villainous black moustache and pointed beard and garbed in the most elaborate kingly styles circa 1515, Powell glowers and menaces most convincingly, and it is obvious that he has thoroughly mastered cinematic technique, never overdoing the gestures and keeping his expressions natural while appropriately expressive. One reviewer wrote, "Mr. William H. Powell, lately of the theatre, makes a fascinating heavy."

Forrest Stanley and Davies put Powell, as the King, temporarily out of commission so that they can make their escape. *(When Knighthood Was in Flower)*

38

OUTCAST

1922 PARAMOUNT

CAST:

Elsie Ferguson *(Miriam)*; David Powell *(Geoffrey Sherwood)*; William David *(Tony Hewlitt)*; Mary Mac-Laren *(Valentine Moreland)*; Charles Wellesley *(John Moreland)*; William Powell *(DeValle)*; Teddy Sampson *(Nellie Essex)*.

CREDITS:

Chet Withey (Director); Josephine Lovett (Scenario); based on the 1914 play *Outcast*, by Herbert Henry Davies.

Running time, 7 reels. Released December 1922.

ESSAY

Elsie Ferguson, who in 1922 was a silent star of some note, had originally enjoyed a huge success in the stage version of *Outcast*, a 1914 play by Hubert Henry Davies. But her 1922 film rendition was less than a success, with *Photoplay's* review setting the tone.

"Elsie Ferguson's *Outcast* on the stage was

Elsie Ferguson doesn't seem to take to Powell's advances. *(Outcast)*

the best performance of her career," the *Photoplay* reviewer wrote, "[but] alas, her film version is highly disappointing. . . . It has been made censor-proof, with appalling results. The star's performance wavers badly."

In yet another of those prostitute-redeemed-by-the-love-of-a-decent-guy tales, Ferguson was supported by the likes of David Powell (as "decent-guy" Geoffrey Sherwood), Mary MacLaren, Charles Wellesley—and William Powell, in a minor, highly thankless role as De Valle, one of the men with whom Ferguson dallies in her streetwalker phase. Again Powell is photographed as swarthy and slimy, written as sinister and racy—and promptly dismissed from the major goings-on. Nonetheless, he made a good impression in this, with his unusual (for the time) looks and oily, assured manner lending themselves well to dark goings-on. It was after this picture that Powell decided to permanently abandon the stage.

Outcast was remade in 1928 under the direction of William A. Seiter (the also-ran Chet Withey guided the 1922 picture with indifferent results) and fared somewhat better with Corinne Griffith and Edmund Lowe starred; for one thing, Agnes Christine Johnston injected more realistic bite and sophistication into the script (harking back to the 1914 stage original) than Josephine Lovett had been able to do in 1922—due largely to the heavy censorship (on and off screen) that assailed the screen medium after Will Hays's clean-up outfit took over in the wake of the Fatty Arbuckle and William Desmond Taylor scandals. (*Photoplay* considered the 1928 retread "daring, well-directed and interesting.")

The story has Ferguson a prostitute down on her luck rescued by David Powell, who is nursing a broken heart because his beloved (Mary MacLaren) has married someone else. MacLaren veers toward him yet again, but Ferguson, who has fallen in love with him, manages to prove she is the better woman—and of course, she wins the guy.

Scheming with Jetta Goudal. (*The Bright Shawl*)

THE BRIGHT SHAWL

1923 INSPIRATION PICTURES

CAST:

Richard Barthelmess (*Charles Abbott, an American*); Edward G. Robinson (*Domingo Escobar, a Cuban Patriot*); Andre Beranger (*Andres*); Mary Astor (*Narcissa Escobar*); William Powell (*Gaspar de Vaca*); Dorothy Gish (*La Clavel*); Jetta Goudal (*La Pilar*); George Humbert (*Jaime Quintara*); Margaret Seddon (*Carmenita Escobar*); Luis Alberni (*Vincente*).

CREDITS:

John S. Robertson (Director); Charles H. Duell (Producer); Edmund Goulding (Scenario); based on the novel by Joseph Hergesheimer; George

Spooning with Mary Astor while Barthelmess muses. (*The Bright Shawl*)

Folsey (Photographer); Everett Shin (Art Director); William Hamilton (Editor).

Running time, 8 reels. Released April 1923.

ESSAY

Photoplay called *The Bright Shawl* "a pretty play of distinct atmospheric charm, a tale of Havana intrigue with Cuban strugglers for liberty on one side and soldiers of Spanish oppression on the other. Well acted by Richard Barthelmess, Dorothy Gish, Jetta Goudal and William Powell."

Richard Barthelmess was the star of this Inspiration Pictures Production and at first, as Powell recalled, they didn't seem to care for one another; but during the trip down to the Cuban locations, they discovered mutual interests and a firm lifetime friendship was formed. In later years Barthelmess, Powell and Ronald Colman would enjoy a one-for-all-and-all-for-one intimate association.

Directed by John S. Robertson, and with an Edmund Goulding scenario adapted from the Joseph Hergesheimer novel, *The Bright Shawl* dealt with Barthelmess's journey to Cuba, where he forms friendships with the rebels

Dorothy Gish ignores Powell's toast. (*The Bright Shawl*)

scenes with Barthelmess, Jetta Goudal, Dorothy Gish and others, and gives a well-thought-out interpretation of the Spanish military mind as it expressed itself in the Cuba of that era. Billed in this as William Powell, he won the praise of critics for his poised demeanor and flashing style. He also got to wear some striking Spanish uniforms to go with his trim moustache and tiny dimple-goatee.

UNDER THE RED ROBE

1923 COSMOPOLITAN–GOLDWYN

CAST:

Robert B. Mantell *(Cardinal Richelieu);* Alma Rubens *(Renée de Cocheforet);* Otto Kruger *(Henri de Cocheforet);* John Charles Thomas *(Gil De Berault);* William H. Powell *(Duke D'Orleans);* Ian MacLaren *(King Louis XIII);* Genevieve Hamper *(Duchesse de Chevreuse);* Mary MacLaren *(Anne of Austria);* Gustav von Seyffertitz *(Clon);* Charles Judels *(Antoine);* Sidney Herbert *(Father Joseph);* Arthur Houseman *(Captain La Rolle).*

CREDITS:

Alan Crosland (Director); Bayard Veiller (Scenario); based on the novel *Under The Red Robe* by Stanley J. Weyman; Harold Wenstrom, Gilbert Warrenton (Photographers); Joseph Urban (Sets); William Frederick Peters (Music).

Running time, 10 reels. Released November 1923.

ESSAY

"Beautifully mounted and costumed, but a bit draggy," was *Photoplay*'s James R. Quirk's pronouncement on the lavish epic of the Louis XIII period, *Under The Red Robe,* which Cosmopolitan Pictures unveiled with a flourish in late 1923.

This time Powell was the Duc D'Orleans, a slimy villain (slimy villains were to become his

Rubens pleads with Mantell as Powell looks on from the right. *(Under the Red Robe)*

specialty throughout the 1920's) who plots the downfall of the king's chief minister, Cardinal Richelieu (played by the famous star of the stage, Robert B. Mantell).

As directed by Alan Crosland with elaborate sets by the famous Joseph Urban, and lavish and painstaking photography by Harold Wenstrom and Gilbert Warrenton, the effort emerged, with critics and the public, as a lavish misfire. Some of the reviewers, however, citing the handsome accoutrements and careful mounting, were more than happy to give the unwieldy venture an "A" for sincere effort.

Powell was William *H.* Powell in the cast listing for this, and the cast was impressive, boasting, besides Mantell, John Charles Thomas (the star, if the length and quality of his role was any indication), Alma Rubens, then one of the screen's reigning beauties, Otto Kruger (later a prominent character actor of the sound era) and Mary MacLaren.

The longwinded plot, based on the 1894 play by Stanley Weyman, had hero Thomas in pursuit of villainous Kruger, who is in rebel-

43

lion against the king and Richelieu. After Kruger is captured, Thomas falls in love with Rubens, Kruger's lovely sister, and returns to Richelieu without his captive, having been reluctant to hurt his lady love.

Meanwhile, at the palace, Powell's Duc D'Orleans has succeeded in getting Richelieu dismissed, but his treachery is exposed by Thomas, and the cardinal is eventually restored to his post and Powell cast into discredit.

All this was told with much grandeur and sweep, but story problems and Crosland's at times faltering direction caused it to bog down at crucial points. But it did give Powell some brief but telling scenes.

Powell duels on horseback with a rival. (*Under the Red Robe*)

44

DANGEROUS MONEY

1924 PARAMOUNT

CAST:

Bebe Daniels *(Adele Clark);* Tom Moore *(Tim Sullivan);* William Powell *(Prince Arnolfo da Pescia);* Dolores Cassinelli *(Signorina Vitale);* Mary Foy *("Auntie" Clark);* Edward O'Connor *(Sheamus Sullivan);* Charles Slattery *(O'Hara);* Peter Lang *(Judge Daniel Orcutt).*

CREDITS:

Frank Tuttle (Director); Adolph Zukor, Jesse L. Lasky (Producers); Julie Herne (Scenario); John Russell (Adapter); from *Clark's Field,* by Robert Herrick; Roy Hunt (Photographer).

Running time, 8 reels. Released October 1924.

ESSAY

Dangerous Money was made after *Romola* but released before it, in October 1924. This was to represent the first pairing of Powell with the popular silent star, Bebe Daniels, with whom he was to do a number of entertaining pictures during the 1920's. *Dangerous Money* was Daniels's first officially starring film, and Tom Moore of the famous Moore Brothers (Owen and Matt were the other two) was her leading man, with Powell on hand as a colorful villain, a fortune-hunting Italian prince. He told an interviewer at the time: "It is strange how my looks lend themselves to Southern European characterizations when I'm actually American as apple pie. But I suppose I should be grateful that my looks increase my range of parts."

Another of those rags-to-riches dramas, this one has Daniels as a slavey in a boarding house who suddenly finds herself the heiress of some New York prime real estate. Next

Italian count Powell makes a sinisterly dapper husband for naïve heiress Daniels. *(Dangerous Money)*

At an Italian carnival, oily count Powell overwhelms his foil, Daniels. *(Dangerous Money)*

Daniels looks scared but Powell persists with the hand-kissing routine. *(Dangerous Money)*

comes finishing school and a European tour with her sweetheart, Tom Moore.

Money goes to Daniels's head, and soon she is jazzing it up with the European fast set, with Moore growing disgusted with her and returning home to America. Soon she is involved with an impoverished prince, Powell, who is up to no good. They marry and Powell starts living off her money. Suddenly they are forced back to New York when, in one of those outlandish plot turns typical of the period, it turns out that her ex-fiancé, Moore, is the true heir to the New York property.

This sets up a situation whereby nefarious Prince da Pescia (Powell) tries to steal the will naming Moore the heir, and for his pains dies a flaming death in a hotel fire. Moore and Daniels proceed to solve the inheritance problem by marrying.

Powell perfected his oily technique as a villainous Italian aristocrat here, bulging out his already bulgy eyes and affecting precious gestures and snazzy continental attire. One reviewer called him "the snazziest foreign villain to show up in films since we don't know when."

Gene Dumont and Powell glare while hapless Daniels kibitzes nervously. *(Dangerous Money)*

ROMOLA

1924 INSPIRATION—METRO GOLDWYN

CAST:

Lillian Gish *(Romola);* Dorothy Gish *(Tessa);* William H. Powell *(Tito Melema);* Ronald Colman *(Carlo Bucellini);* Charles Lane *(Baldassar Calve);* Herbert Grimwood *(Savonarola);* Bonaventura Ibanez *(Bardo Bardi);* Frank Puglia *(Adolfo Spini);* Amelia Summerville *(Brigida);* Tina Ceccaci Renaldi *(Monna Ghita);* Eduilio Mucci *(Nello);* Angela Scatigna *(Bratti);* Ugo Uccellini *(Bishop of Nemours);* Alfredo Martinelli *(Captain of the Barque);* Attilo Deodati *(Tomaso).*

CREDITS:

Henry King (Director); Will M. Ritchey (Screenplay); adapted from the novel by George Eliot; Jules Furthman and Don Bartlett (Titles); Louis H. Gottschalk (Music); Robert Haas (Art Director); Roy Overbaugh, William Schurr, Ferdinand Risi (Photographers); Duncan Mansfield (Editor).

Running time, 11 reels. Released December 1924.

ESSAY

Powell, still listed as William *H.* Powell, joined Lillian and Dorothy Gish and Ronald Colman in Italy for the filming of one of the famed Gish Sisters' most lavish films, *Romola.* As Tito Melema, Powell had the major male starring role, and while this Melema was hardly an admirable character, he was strongly conceived by the screenwriters, who based the screenplay on George Eliot's historical romance of 1862.

Powell was most impressed with the careful mounting of *Romola* in Italy and the fine, meticulous direction of Henry King, found the Gishes a joy to work with, and formed a fast and permanent friendship with Ronald

Lillian Gish and Powell face an intruder at their banquet table. *(Romola)*

Colman, whose role in this was actually far smaller than his own.

In Florence, the Powell character marries Lillian Gish for power, as she is the daughter of a blind but influential scholar. With the assistance of scheming Frank Puglia, Powell becomes the leading magistrate in the city. After that his villainies multiply. He seduces Dorothy Gish, an innocent peasant girl, via a mock marriage, and among other iniquities sentences to death Savonarola (Herbert Grim-

Powell and Lillian Gish emerge from the church. *(Romola)*

Powell makes sly overtures to innocent peasant girl Dorothy Gish. *(Romola)*

wood), the beloved hero of the people of Florence.

The people rise in rebellion against Powell and he winds up drowned in the river. Lillian Gish's character finds that of Dorothy Gish, and the wronged wife cares tenderly for the betrayed girl. Eventually Lillian's Romola finds happiness with Colman, a talented sculptor, who has loved her for a long time.

Lillian Gish has always defended *Romola* from the numerous critics who assailed the picture for its handsome lifelessness. *Photoplay*'s James R. Quirk had strong reservations about it, writing: "George Eliot's novel proves a poor vehicle for the Gish sisters, [with] elaborate Florentine settings but little human interest."

Though the Gishes gave superb acting performances, and Colman was effective in his small role, it was Powell who had the juiciest role and emerged from the picture to best advantage. He always was to retain fond memories of it, and thought it a dignified, beautiful film. His was the only role, unfortunately, with true dimension. "A handsome, stately bore" summed up the reaction of most critics.

Lillian Gish clings to treacherous Powell's hand. *(Romola)*

TOO MANY KISSES

1925 PARAMOUNT

CAST:

Richard Dix *(Richard Gaylord, Jr.);* Frances Howard *(Yvonne Hurja);* William Powell *(Julio);* Frank Currier *(Richard Gaylord, Sr.);* Joseph Burke *(Mr. Simmons);* Albert Tavernier *(Manuel Hurja);* Arthur Ludwig *(Miguel);* Paul Panzer *(Pedro);* Harpo Marx *(The Village Peter Pan);* Alyce Mills *(Flapper).*

CREDITS:

Paul Sloane (Director); Adolph Zukor, Jesse L. Lasky (Producers); Gerald Duffy (Scenario); based on the *Cosmopolitan* story by John Monk Saunders; Hal Rosson (Photographer).

Running time, 6 reels. Released January 1925.

ESSAY

In *Too Many Kisses,* Powell's first 1925 release, he reinforced his growing reputation as the movies' villain-with-a-different-quality. Richard Dix, the film's star, was so impressed with Powell's work in *Dangerous Money* and other films, that he expressly requested him.

Too Many Kisses was distinguished by the presence of two people who were to figure importantly in Hollywood's future. Frances Howard, who had come to the films from Broadway and was Dix's leading lady in this, was to become the second wife of Sam Goldwyn that same year, 1925, and would help him actively to shape the great films of Goldwyn's later period. Their son, Samuel Goldwyn, Jr., born in 1926, was also to become a producer. The other later-prominent figure to be seen in *Too Many Kisses* was Harpo Marx, who did a solo as "The Village Peter Pan" of a Basque community; this was to be his first film, and he did not do another until

Dix's American fisticuffs more than match Powell's Basque knifing skills. *(Too Many Kisses)*

he joined his brothers four years later in their first film, *The Cocoanuts* (1929).

Based on a John Monk Saunders *Cosmopolitan* story in 1923, *Too Many Kisses* dealt with a spoiled playboy, Richard Dix, who is sent by his father to Spain to cure his womanizing. The father has the impression that the Basque women of Spain never marry outside of their own race, so he feels Dix will have scant pickings there.

Soon Dix finds himself in a triangle including Yvonne (Howard) who is coveted by Julio (Powell) a Civil Guard officer. After refusing to fight a duel with Powell, due to his promise to Howard, Dix is kidnapped and taken to the mountains by Powell's men. Powell tries to secure Howard's hand in marriage, but the escaping Dix confronts him at a festival where knife-throwing gives way to fisticuffs at which American Dix is expert and basque Powell not-so-hot.

With typical plot illogic, at this point Dix's father (Frank Currier) shows up fortuitously and not only approves of his love for Howard but takes him into the family business.

Of all this, one reviewer said, "Powell, an American, plays a Basque villain better than any Basque original could; Dix makes a nice

49

foil for him; their acting styles contrast interestingly."

FAINT PERFUME

1925 PARAMOUNT–
B. P. SCHULBERG

CAST:

Seena Owen *(Richmiel Crumb);* William Powell *(Barnaby Powers);* Alyce Mills *(Ledda Perrin);* Mary Alden *(Ma Crumb);* Russell Simpson *(Grandpa Crumb);* Betty Francisco *(Pearl Crumb);* Jacqueline Saunders *(Tweet Crumb);* Philo McCullough *(Rich-miel's lover);* Ned Sparks *(Orrin Crumb);* Dicky Brandon *(Oliver Powers);* Joan Standing *(The Hired Girl).*

CREDITS:

Louis Gasnier (Director); B. P. Schulberg (Producer); John Goodrich (Scenario); adapted from *Faint Perfume* by Zona Gale; Allen Siegler (Photographer).

Running time, 6 reels. Released June 1925.

ESSAY

Faint Perfume had the misfortune to be one of the 1925 movies that *Photoplay*'s James R. Quirk picked to review at random, and his individual reaction was typical of the stiletto-ish approach of his magazine's reviewing stance where poor movies were concerned. Of

Powell doesn't feel that wife Seena Owen is much of a mother to son Dicky Brandon. *(Faint Perfume)*

this effort he wrote: "Faint is right. A jumbled, movieized version of Zona Gale's excellent novel." Quirk did tell producer B. P. Schulberg (father of the later-famous writer Budd) that Powell in his opinion was one of the best actors who had come down the movie pike—and this three years before Powell's excellent voice shot him to real stardom.

Powell was cast sympathetically by Schulberg in this, thus establishing an image contrasting with his usual villainous incarnations—and in the process winning new admirers via his demonstrated versatility. Zona Gale had written one of her usual psychologically adept, characterizationally sharp novels, but as adapted by John Goodrich for the screen and directed by Louis Gasnier it emerged as pretty watered-down—nor was the plot the freshest.

Powell, married for six years to Seena Owen, a flighty, irresponsible type, and the father of a five-year-old boy, Dicky Brandon, decides he wants a divorce. Owen takes the boy back with her to her parents' home. Feeling that she is not the best influence on the boy, Powell follows her to ask for custody. There he proceeds to fall in love with Alyce Mills, Owen's nice-girl cousin, who represents to Powell the warmth, womanliness and stability that his ex-wife notoriously lacks.

When Owen finds out what is going on, she spitefully refuses her husband custody of the boy, and there are hurt feelings all around. The boy almost dies in an accident, and Owen, now interested in another man, decides to go off with him and leave the boy to Powell and Mills.

Seena Owen has the odd name of "Richmiel," while Alyce Mills has the more euphoniously positive name "Ledda." Powell is inexplicably stuck with the name "Barnaby" and the kid is "Oliver." Most critics agreed with Quirk on this, with one trade writer stating: "Nice demonstration of Powell's versatility but little else."

MY LADY'S LIPS

1925 PARAMOUNT— B. P. SCHULBERG

CAST:

Alyce Mills (*Dora Blake*); William Powell (*Scott Seddon*); Clara Bow (*Lola Lombard*); Frank Keenan (*Forbes Lombard*); Ford Sterling (*Smike*); Gertrude Short (*A Crook*); Matthew Betz (*Eddie Gault*); John Sainpolis (*Inspector*).

CREDITS:

James P. Hogan (Director); B. P. Schulberg (Producer); John Goodrich (Screenplay); from Goodrich's original Story; Allen Siegler (Photographer).

Running time, 7 reels. Released July 1925.

ESSAY

My Lady's Lips cast Powell for the first time with Clara Bow, whose producer-mentor, B. P. Schulberg, had been grooming her for some time. When Schulberg rejoined Paramount in 1925 after a period of independent producing, he took Bow with him, and she began her rise as the gal of superior esprit and exceptional energy who led with her heart more than was good for her. In *My Lady's Lips*, directed by James Hogan with a script by John Goodrich, Bow is a spoiled good-time-type daughter of a newspaper editor who gets involved with a gambling ring. Powell is the paper's star reporter who infiltrates the gang to get a top story. There he falls in love with gang leader Alyce Mills. The police raid the gambling premises and reporter-posing-as-crook Powell is captured with Mills during an escape attempt. After a tough interrogation by police, they both sign confessions. Prison is the result for Powell, but after his release he and Mills find that true natural love is a re-

Naughty girl Clara Bow demonstrates the lips in question. *(This is the only still from this picture to be found anywhere.) (Too Many Kisses)*

demptive factor despite her continuing predilection for games of chance.

Schulberg took Powell to Hollywood for this film, on a one-shot deal, and though he disliked leaving his wife and new son in New York, Powell took the role because Schulberg for the second time was offering him a change of pace from the villain roles he had been typed in.

Schulberg talked up Powell to the Paramount bosses with whom he, Schulberg, had by then reaffiliated, and the impression Powell made in *My Lady's Lips* would eventually win him a long-term Paramount–Famous Players Lasky contract.

James Hogan was a director who did his work without frills, and while his over-all product was never to be distinguished, he did keep things moving and lively. *Photoplay* was ambivalent in its review, calling *My Lady's Lips* "a crook melodrama that is lively and often amusing, but we dare you to try to believe in the plot."

Powell found the West Coast, with its perpetual sunshine and leisurely pace a sharp contrast with New York, but its good weather and prime film-making facilities were in time responsible for making it the main American moviemaking spot. Already, Powell was contemplating a move to Hollywood; on balance, he felt, it was the best place to be.

THE BEAUTIFUL CITY

1925 INSPIRATION–FIRST NATIONAL

CAST:

Richard Barthelmess *(Tony Gillardi);* Dorothy Gish *(Mollie);* William Powell *(Nick Di Silva);* Frank Puglia *(Carlo Gillardi);* Florence Auer *(Mamma Gillardi);* Lassie Bronte *(Dog).*

CREDITS:

Kenneth Webb (Director); Edmund Goulding (Story); Don Bartlett, C. Graham Baker (Scenario); Roy Overbaugh, Stuart Nelson (Photographers); William Hamilton (Editor).

Running time, 7 reels. Released October, 1925

ESSAY

Richard Barthelmess, who had formed a fast friendship with Powell during the making of *The Bright Shawl*, was set in mid-1925 to do a film with Dorothy Gish, *The Beautiful City*, for Inspiration Pictures. The film was to be shot largely on New York's lower East Side. He felt that Powell would be perfect for the heavy, an Italian gangster; he asked for him, and got him. Powell was delighted to be working again with Barthelmess and also with Dorothy Gish, who along with her sister Lillian had had such a pleasant and rewarding association with him during the making of *Romola*.

Director Kenneth Webb did his best, as did Don Bartlett and C. Graham Baker with the screenplay, but the results were mixed, with *Photoplay* commending the atmospheric tenement district photography on the New York location but declaring also that the picture was not up to the Barthelmess standard. There was praise, however, for Powell's vivid interpretation of Nick Di Silva, and Dorothy Gish and Barthelmess were hailed as touching in their roles. Roy Overbaugh's photographic and atmospheric touches also came in for commendation, but the film is not regarded, in retrospect, as top-drawer Barthelmess or Dorothy Gish. Edmund Goulding, later famous primarily as a director, came up with the original story, which was exciting enough.

Barthelmess is a young Italian flower vendor who must take second place to his flashier brother, Frank Puglia, who is their mother's favorite. Gish is his girlfriend, of Irish extraction, who loves and believes in Barthelmess despite his misfortunes.

Powell is a domineering racketeer who has taken over Puglia's life, however, and when they engineer a major robbery, the self-sacrificing Barthelmess, to protect his mother from the truth, takes the blame and does a jail term. When he gets out, he is forced to save his brother yet again from Powell's evil influence; his mother gets shot by Powell, who then falls accidentally to his death. The mother

Powell was delighted to be working again with his friends Gish and Barthelmess.

recovers, Barthelmess and Gish make plans to marry, and on a boat trip past the Battery, Barthelmess, now happy and at peace, again surveys the "Beauty" of his "City." Powell said at the time he considered his role as written "vivid" and his reuniting with his co-stars "a privilege." Ten years later he would be a bigger star than either.

53

WHITE MICE

1926 PINELLAS FILMS– ASSOCIATED EXHIBITORS

CAST:

Jacqueline Logan *(Inez Rojas);* William Powell *(Roddy Forrester);* Ernest Hilliard *(Colonel Vega);* Bigelow Cooper *(R.B. Forrester);* Lucius Henderson *(General Rojas);* Marie Burke *(Senora Rojas);* Harlan Knight *(MacKildrick);* Reginald Sheffield *(Peter de Peyster);* F. Vaux Wilson *(Dr. Vicenti);* William Wadsworth *(Sylvanus Codman);* Richard Lee *(Ma-nuel);* George De Richelevie *(El Comandante);* Vivian Vernon *(La Borrachita).*

CREDITS:

Edward H. Griffith (Director); Royal W. Wetherald (Producer); Randolph Bartlett (Scenario and Adaptation); based on *White Mice* (1909) by Richard Harding Davis; Marcel Le Picard (Photographer).

Running time, 6 reels. Released January 1926.

ESSAY

Director Edward H. Griffith's films were called by one critic "competently directed but mostly routine." One of the most "routine" of his silents was *White Mice,* Powell's first 1926 release. It was a picture he did for an independent of modest pretensions, Pinellas Films,

Powell *(at right, clean shaven)* and Jacqueline Logan rescue her father (Lucius Henderson) from prison. *(White Mice)*

54

headed by one Royal W. Wetherald, releasing through Associated Exhibitors.

"It is nice to see the nefarious Mr. Powell of the dastardly deeds functioning as a good guy in this," one reviewer commented, adding, "He can fit on a hero's glove as snugly as he does that of a villain." Powell was *sans* moustache in this.

As adapted by Randolph Bartlett, a James R. Quirk protégé who had gone from *Photoplay* to screenwriting, this version of Richard Harding Davis's 1909 piece had Powell as Roddy Forrester, who is a charter member of an idealistic outfit called The White Mice Club, which specializes in getting assorted people out of jams of all kinds.

Powell's father, Bigelow Cooper, dispatches him to a Latin American republic and there he gets romantic with Jacqueline Logan, daughter of the republic's much-admired president, Lucius Henderson. When Powell learns that the president is actually languishing in prison, he swears by the White Mice that he will free him. After variegated trials, he succeeds in liberating the president, and wins the love of his daughter.

White Mice, while modestly produced and indifferently mounted and distributed, did give Powell a chance, at age 33, to demonstrate that he could swashbuckle and derring-do heroically with the best of them. In a role equally suited to Richard Barthelmess or Richard Dix, he showed just how versatile and convincing an actor he could be. Reportedly, when his close pal Barthelmess heard about his role in this picture, he joshed him with, "Hey, you're trying to crowd *my* territory!"

Because of its weak distribution, *White Mice* got little critical notice, but what little there was favored Powell's efforts.

SEA HORSES

1926 PARAMOUNT

CAST:

Jack Holt *(George Glanville);* Florence Vidor *(Helen Salvia);* William Powell *(Lorenzo Salvia);* George Bancroft *(Cochran);* Mack Swain *(Bimbo-Bomba);* Frank Campeau *(Senor Cordoza);* Allan Simpson *(Harvey);* George Nichols *(Marx);* Mary Dow *(Cina Salvia);* Dick La Reno *(Henry);* Frank Austin *(Cheadle).*

Powell makes Vidor the worst of husbands. *(Sea Horses)*

CREDITS:

Allan Dwan (Director); Adolph Zukor, Jesse L. Lasky (Producers); James Shelley Hamilton (Screenplay); based on "Sea Horses" by Francis Brett Young; Becky Gardiner (Adaptation); James Wong Howe (Photographer).

Running time, 7 reels. Released February 1926.

ESSAY

In its 1926 review, *Photoplay* said of *Sea Horses:* "Fair stuff because of the presence of Florence Vidor in the cast. Not as snappy as the usual Allan Dwan production."

In this Paramount release, Powell found himself up against the likes of Jack Holt, a prime Man of Action, and George Bancroft, then on his rise to stardom as "a rough character with human overtones," as one critic called him. Florence Vidor was one of the screen's loveliest stars of the time, greatly given to suffering and assorted mistreatments at the hands of the male. Powell's role was a rather thankless one, and he was a far cry from the hero he was allowed to be in *White Mice.* The heroics all went to Holt and Bancroft.

Vidor has been deserted by her Italian husband, Powell, who has left her with a small daughter. A year later she boards ship for an East African port where he is now located. On board she meets Holt, the captain, Bancroft, the first mate, and third officer Allan Simpson. Bancroft and Simpson court her openly, while Holt sulks manfully in the background.

At the East African port, Vidor, to her horror, discovers that her husband, Powell, has been reduced to a drunken weakling and derelict. He gets money from Holt in exchange for her freedom, whereupon Vidor flees the ship, resists an attack by the drunken Powell, gets caught in a typhoon, almost loses her child to Powell, is rescued yet again by Holt after Bancroft and Powell kill each other off—and finally gets safely back to England with Holt.

The rather busy plot, based on a Francis Brett Young piece, seemed to irritate most of the critics, several of whom opined that Powell was wasted in his irredeemably mountebankish role, that the Holt-Bancroft heroics were on the static side this time around, and that director Allan Dwan was not up to his usual form.

Powell later said of his role, "It was as low-down as I could get—and that was low indeed, in more ways than one."

DESERT GOLD
1926 PARAMOUNT

Neil Hamilton, George Rigas, Robert Frazer and Powell clown on the set. *(Desert Gold)*

CAST:

Neil Hamilton *(George Thorne);* Shirley Mason *(Mercedes Castanada);* Robert Frazer *(Dick Gale);* William Powell *(Landree);* Josef Swickard *(Sebastian Castaneda);* George Irving *(Richard Stanton Gale);* Eddie Gribbon *(One-Round Kelley);* Frank Lackteen *(Yaqui);* Richard Howard *(Sergeant);* Bernard Siegel *(Goat Herder);* Aline Goodwin *(Alarcon's Wife);* Ralph Yearsley *(Halfwit);* George Rigas *(Verd).*

CREDITS:

George B. Seitz (Director); Adolph Zukor, Jesse L. Lasky (Producers): Hector Turnbull, B.P. Schulberg (Supervisors); based on a novel by Zane Grey; Lucien Hubbard (Scenario); Charles Edgar Schoenbaum (Photographer).

Running time, 7 reels. Released March 1926.

ESSAY

The works of Zane Grey, the Western Adventure novelist, were popular film fare in the 1920's, and Powell essayed one of Grey's standard Western villains in *Desert Gold.* For this role he went dirty-faced and unshaven in a ten-gallon hat, as Landree, "an unscrupulous outlaw and killer."

On hand for the standard heroics are Neil Hamilton and Robert Frazer, and Shirley Mason is the heroine over whom the boys vie. Frazer, spoiled playboy son of a strait-laced Eastern family, has come West to help his friend Hamilton, an Army lieutenant, on the Mexican border. There they combat the nefarious doings of Powell, who has plundered Shirley Mason's father's villa and attempts to abduct the girl herself.

Mason escapes and flees with Frazer into the desert. There are sandstorms, landslides, and whatnot, with Hamilton, who is also in love with Mason, rescuing the party. Powell's villainous plans are permanently thwarted thanks to an Indian's heroism, and Hamilton chivalrously gives up the girl to pal Frazee, knowing that she loves the latter.

Powell, though cast as the usual villain, felt

that this role gave him some swashbuckling range, as he had to hop on horses, sashay about the desert, get good and dirty and dusty, flash his eyes and scowl in his best sinister fashion.

He was to say about this time, "I don't want to play villains exclusively, of course, but there is a certain vitality to a villain; he shoots off sparks and the audience is always watching him, wondering what he will do next. In fact, they watch him more than they do the hero! And that's not so bad a share of the attention."

Photoplay felt that *Desert Gold* was only "fair." Many publications ignored it, but one cited its "busy carnage" and called Powell "vitally villainous."

THE RUNAWAY

1926 PARAMOUNT

CAST:

Clara Bow *(Cynthia Meade);* Warner Baxter *(Wade Murrell);* William Powell *(Jack Harrison);* George Bancroft *(Lesher Skidmore);* Edythe Chapman *(Wade's Mother).*

CREDITS:

William C. DeMille (Director); Adolph Zukor, Jesse L. Lasky (Producers); Albert Shelby LeVino (Adaptation); based on the novel *The Flight to the Hills* by Charles Neville Buck; Charles Boyle (Photographer).

Running time, 7 reels. Released April 1926.

ESSAY

Powell was teamed again with the ebullient Clara Bow in *The Runaway,* which profited from the careful direction of William C. DeMille and a well-crafted scenario based on Charles Neville Buck's novel, *The Flight to the Hills.*

Powell and Bow, who are affianced, are

working on a movie set where she is an actress. They are on location in Tennessee. She shoots him accidentally during a movie scene, and fearful she has killed him, she flees. Coming under the protection[1] of a mountaineer, Warner Baxter, who helps her escape into Kentucky, she goes to his home. There love develops between them.

As an added plot twist, the other mountaineers in the primitive community disapprove of Bow, considering her a fast "painted woman," and Baxter is obliged to defend her. Bow

Powell lures Bow in for some firewater. (*The Runaway*)

58

The sophisticated pair toast each other. *(The Runaway)*

becomes accustomed to mountain ways, though she demurs at accepting Baxter's love for fear her "murderess" status will ruin any life they might have together.

Suddenly Powell reappears. It seems he was only slightly wounded, and he sets out to win Bow back, recalling to her his sophisticated city ways as compared to the primitive conditions in the mountain community. He and Baxter become friends, and he even saves Baxter's life during a skirmish. Bow is torn between the two men, but it is Baxter she loves, and eventually she chooses him.

Bow and Powell get a lot of sophisticated big-city badinage into the film, especially in their early scenes together before the accident, and Powell manages to be so charming and colorful in his rendition that more than one critic wondered out loud why Bow, portrayed as a good-time, fast-lane gal in the

Peppy Bow practices her wiles on thoughtful Powell. *(The Runaway)*

Powell tries to talk Bow back to the Bright Lights. *(The Runaway)*

A wistful Baxter worries that Powell has taken back his girl. *(The Runaway)*

opening scenes, would eventually choose an unlettered Kentuckian, however handsome and well-meaning, over a man so obviously more suited to her.

"Powell and Bow do very well together," one critic wrote, "and both are obviously headed for bigger things." This was one of Bow's first starring pictures; the next few years were to take her to the top as the "It" Girl. Powell later recalled her "personality" and "pep."

ALOMA OF THE SOUTH SEAS

1926 PARAMOUNT

CAST:

Gilda Gray *(Aloma);* Percy Marmont *(Bob Holden);* Warner Baxter *(Nuitane);* William Powell *(Van Templeton);* Harry Morey *(Red Malloy);* Julanne Johnston *(Sylvia);* Joseph Smiley *(Andrew Taylor);* Frank

Montgomery *(Hongi);* Madame Burani *(Hina);* Ernestine Gaines *(Taula);* Aurelio Coccia *(Sailor).*

CREDITS:

Maurice Tourneur (Director); Adolph Zukor, Jesse L. Lasky (Producers); E. Lloyd Sheldon (Supervising Editor); James Creelman (Scenario and Adaptation); Charles M. Kirk (Art Director); Harry Fischbeck (Photographer).

Running time, 9 reels. Released May 1926.

ESSAY

Aloma of the South Seas capitalized on the mid-1920's craze for everything Hawaiian, including the dances, the music and the instrument (ukulele.) In 1925, the play had captivated Broadway, and in 1926 Paramount produced it under Maurice Tourneur's direction, with the "Queen of the Shimmy," Gilda Gray, who on the stage had made her fortune via the distinctive dance which was forevermore to be associated with her name.

Gilda was more of a dancer than an actress, as her short career in films attested, but her limitations were disguised by the protective powerhouse contingent of seasoned actors

Powell applies his lewd addresses to the native girls. (*Aloma of the South Seas*)

who were put in support of her, including Powell (in yet another slimy-mountebank role), Percy Marmont, a popular leading man of the period, and Warner Baxter, who plays the native in love with Gray's Aloma, Julanne Johnston is along for the ride as the white woman who gets mixed up in the confused romantic proceedings on a South Sea island.

It seems that Aloma, possessively loved by Baxter, gets involved with the American Marmont. Along comes Marmont's former American love, Johnston, with her husband, Powell.

Powell looks on ironically as Gray and Marmont embrace. Beside Powell, Julanne Johnston. *(Aloma of the South Seas)*

The latter tries to seduce Aloma-Gray but is repulsed. Meanwhile Marmont, his initial passion for Gray having cooled, returns to Johnston. At the end, the nefarious Powell character is drowned and the Americans and Polynesians are correctly paired off.

Powell had little to do in this other than the standard villain stuff, sneering knowingly at Marmont's pursuit of Gray and rushing in for the kill when opportunity beckons. Based on the play by John Hymer and LeRoy Clemens, *Aloma* was written for the screen by James Creelman, who cinematized the situations wherever he could, his work being complemented by Tourneur's sweepingly authentic feeling for the romance of the locations, which were filmed in Puerto Rico rather than the South Seas where the story situations transpired—but no matter; authentic-looking locales were assiduously hunted-out and employed on the Caribbean island. Gray's far-famed wiggle was not neglected either; the critics concentrated on this rather than her acting attempts.

BEAU GESTE

1926 PARAMOUNT

CAST

Ronald Colman *(Michael "Beau" Geste);* Neil Hamilton *(Digby Geste);* Ralph Forbes *(John Geste);* Alice Joyce *(Lady Patricia Brandon);* Mary Brian *(Isabel);* Noah Beery *(Sergeant Lejaune);* Norman Trevor *(Major de Beaujolais);* William Powell *(Boldini);* George Regas *(Maris);* Bernard Siegel *(Schwartz);* Victor McLaglen *(Hank);* Donald Stewart *(Buddy);* Paul McAllister *(St. Andre);* Redmond Finlay *(Cordere);* Ram Singh *(Prince Ram Singh);* Maurice Mur-

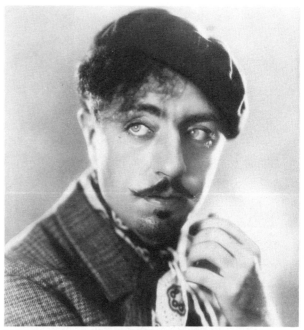

Powell is superb as the slimy villain, Boldini. *(Beau Geste)*

Powell, Forbes, Colman, Hamilton and Beery in a falsely friendly publicity pose. *(Beau Geste)*

phy *("Beau" as a child);* Mickey McBan *(John as a child).*

CREDITS:

Herbert Brenon (Director); Adolph Zukor and Jesse L. Lasky (Producers); a Herbert Brenon Production; Paul Schofield (Screenplay); John Russell and Herbert Brenon (Adaptation); based on the novel by Percival Christopher Wren; J. Roy Hunt (Photographer); Julian Fleming (Art Director); Technicolor Sequences.

Running time, 12 reels. Released August 1926.

ESSAY

Powell had a small but telling role in the famous *Beau Geste,* which was actually a starring film for his friend, Ronald Colman, with whom he had a pleasant reunion when the

Powell eavesdrops on the brothers, hoping to find out about their jewel. *(Beau Geste)*

Powell does some villainous cogitating. *(Beau Geste)*

65

It looks like Colman and Forbes have caught Powell at something less than honorable. *(Beau Geste)*

film was shot in California. In it he played Boldini, a scheming Indian mountebank who seeks to possess a jewel reputed to be in the possession of one of his fellow French Foreign Legionnaires, and who kills himself after being tortured.

Powell made a vivid impression in this story, made from the famous novel by Percival Christopher Wren, a story that was to be made over and over again during the following years, so perennial was its appeal. The rather complicated plot had Colman, Ralph Forbes and Neil Hamilton as brothers who flee England after there is some misunderstanding over the theft of a family heirloom, a jewel. The boys join the French Foreign Legion and there are scuffles with native troops, quarrels with brutal superiors, the death of Beau (Colman) and the revenging of his shooting by his brother. The only one who gets to return to England at long last is Forbes, who is reunited with his lady love, Mary Brian. Alice Joyce, a lovely silent star, also figures in the proceedings.

The sweep and romanticism of the story, its exotic setting, the attachment of the brothers to one another and the depth of their loyalty, the assorted villainies of Powell and Noah

Beery, as the cruel Sergeant Lejaune, the heat of the desert, the valor in the face of adversity—all these elements coalesced into an irresistible box office bonanza that was the smash of 1926.

Colman is his usual romantic self here, delicate of spirit yet masculinely forthright when occasion demands it. He, Forbes, and Hamilton are ably offset by the oily chicaneries of the Powell character; it is regarded as one of Powell's finest acting creations, though his footage is limited. *Photoplay* stated: "Percival Wren's best-seller has been followed with fidelity."

TIN GODS

1926 PARAMOUNT

CAST:

Thomas Meighan *(Roger Drake)*; Renée Adorée *(Carita)*; Aileen Pringle *(Janet Stone)*; William Powell *(Tony Santelli)*; Hale Hamilton *(Dr. McCoy)*; John Harrington *(Dougherty)*; Joe King *(First Foreman)*; Robert E. O'Connor *(Second Foreman)*; Delbert Whitten, Jr. *(Billy)*.

CREDITS:

Allan Dwan *(Director)*; Adolph Zukor, Jesse L. Lasky *(Producers)*; William LeBaron *(Associate Producer)*; James Shelley Hamilton *(Screenplay)*; based on the play by William Anthony McGuire; Paul Dickey, Howard Emmett Rogers *(Adaptation)*; Alvin Wyckoff *(Photographer)*.

Running time, 9 reels. Released September 1926.

ESSAY

Tin Gods was based on the 1923 play by William Anthony McGuire, an Irish-American writer who was having a golden period at that time. Allan Dwan directed with his customary flair, from a screenplay by James Shelley Hamilton. The film starred Thomas Meighan, a top favorite with women ticket-buyers since

66

his romancing of Gloria Swanson in *Male and Female*. Aileen Pringle and Renée Adorée co-starred. Powell was thrown away as a minor character, one Tony Santelli, who is brought in only to provide the appropriate atmosphere and make standard 1926-style grimaces. The picture was all Meighan, Pringle and Adorée.

Photoplay pretty well set the tone for the 1926 reviewers, commenting, in part: "Tommie Meighan needed a good story, director and cast to prove he's still a good actor. Of course Renée Adorée helps to make this interesting." Which is not to infer that *Tin Gods* was any blockbuster. "Pleasant," "nicely acted," "a good evening's entertainment" pretty well summed up the reviews of the time.

An engineer on the rise, but saddled with a wife (Pringle) who in true early-feminist style seeks political office to the neglect of her husband and child, Meighan makes do, after a fashion, until their child has an accident. This causes a separation, and Meighan's subsequent retreat into alcoholism. In South America to construct a bridge, Meighan nearly dies of fever but is rehabilitated by Adorée (borrowed from MGM for this opus). Love builds gradually between them, but when Adorée

Meighan realizes he has lost his true love, Adorée. (*Tin Gods*)

learns that Pringle is seeking a reconciliation after licking her wounds from a political defeat, Adorée jumps from a bridge feeling that Meighan still hankers for his wife.

The film opens and closes with Meighan's regular visits to the chapel he had erected in Adorée's memory. Apart from the emotional confusions and displacements inherent in this film, it is chiefly of interest today for the scandalous waste of Powell's talents in a role that gave him no opportunity to shine.

THE GREAT GATSBY

1926 PARAMOUNT

CAST:

Warner Baxter (*Jay Gatsby*); Lois Wilson (*Daisy Buchanan*); Neil Hamilton (*Nick Carraway*); Georgia Hale (*Myrtle Wilson*); William Powell (*George Wilson*); Hale Hamilton (*Tom Buchanan*); George Nash (*Charles Wolf*); Carmelita Geraghty (*Jordan Baker*); Eric Blore (*Lord Digby*); "Gunboat" Smith (*Bert*); Claire Whitney (*Catherine*).

CREDITS:

Herbert Brenon (Director); Adolph Zukor, Jesse L. Lasky (Producers); Becky Gardiner (Screenplay); Elizabeth Meeham (Adaptation); Leo Tover (Photographer).

Running time, 8 reels. Released November 1926.

ESSAY

F. Scott Fitzgerald's *The Great Gatsby* (1925) is regarded as his greatest work, and the movies have made versions of it over many years, including this 1926 Paramount effort with Warner Baxter as the ill-fated Gatsby, a 1949 repeat with Alan Ladd, and a 1974 version with Robert Redford. Many film students prefer the 1926 version, if only because it was made during the correct period, with an authentic contemporary ambience no out-of-pethe 1926 version: "Fitzgerald's novel, with its unscrupulous hero, violates some pet screen traditions. It's unusual entertainment."

Fans of 1926 also found themselves surprised by the versatility of Powell, who in a minor supporting role got across the greasy, unlettered, elementally homicidal George Wilson, whose visceral feelings triumph over any cerebral cogitations, of which he is obviously incapable.

In the story, which was both a novel by Fitzgerald and a play by Owen Davis (both in the same year, 1925), Baxter in 1917 is a young Army officer in love with society girl Wilson. Nine years later, though he has since lost her to a socialite because his background had proven inferior ("Gatsby" had originally been "Gatz"), he meets her on Long Island. Shady connections have given him spurious wealth and a lavish summer home. Gatsby and Daisy resume their relationship; her husband has meanwhile been carrying on an affair with garage-owner Powell's wife. When Daisy kills the wife in an auto accident, Gatsby takes the blame and is killed by the gone-berserk Powell. The 1926 reviewers called Powell "electric," "brutal" and "unthinkingly animalistic" in his role; it was their way of paying tribute to his consummate versatility in a small but soundly characterized rendition of an obtuse cuckold.

As the cuckolded garage owner, Powell demonstrated his versatility. (*The Great Gatsby*)

riod later conception could match. Also, Baxter, with his half-cocky, half-confused characterization of the on-the-make Gatsby, aspiring to a social station and a girl beyond his reach, is felt to have, in retrospect, the edge on the wooden and inexpressive Alan Ladd in 1949 and the much too pretty and superficially glib Redford a quarter-century after that. Lois Wilson, Betty Field and Mia Farrow respectively played Gatsby's light o' love Daisy Buchanan in the 1926, 1949 and 1974 films. *Photoplay*'s reviewer declared of

NEW YORK

1927 PARAMOUNT

CAST:

Ricardo Cortez (*Michael Angelo Cassidy*); Lois Wilson (*Marjorie Church*); Estelle Taylor (*Angie Miller*); William Powell (*Trent Regan*); Norman Trevor (*Randolph Church*); Richard "Skeets" Gallagher (*Buck*); Margaret Quimby (*Helen Matthews*); Lester Schariff (*Izzy Blumenstein*); Charles Byer (*Jimmie Wharton*).

CREDITS

Luther Reed (Director); Adolph Zukor, Jesse L. Lasky (Producers); William LeBaron (Associate Producer); Becky Gardiner (Original Story); Barbara Chambers (Co-author, Original Story); Forrest Halsey (Screenplay); J. Roy Hunt (Photographer).

Running time, 7 reels. Released February 1927.

ESSAY

"Trite and obvious," *Photoplay* called *New York,* which was shot on actual Manhattan locations such as the Bowery. Ricardo Cortez, Lois Wilson and Estelle Taylor were the other principal actors involved with Powell, in a film directed by Luther Reed.

Powell, however, garnered some good reviews cross-country as Trent Regan, who has risen from the streets to gangsterism. Shot at the Astoria studios and on location, the story deals with four old friends who regularly meet at a Bowery café that has special associations for them. Ricardo Cortez has gone into business (show business, that is) as a drummer-composer; Lester Schariff is climbing in politics; "Skeets" Gallagher is a musical arranger;

and Powell does the criminal dirty work, with fierce, easily aroused temper to boot.

Though taken with Cortez, Estelle Taylor winds up with Powell, for reasons never fully elucidated by the screenplay. Cortez winds up with a society girl, Lois Wilson. Imagining that his wife has been unfaithful with Cortez, although she was only visiting him innocently, Powell shoots her. Cortez, though innocent, is convicted of the murder, but Powell is finally unmasked as the perpetrator.

All this was gotten across by director Reed in a fast-paced, "New Yorky" style, but many reviewers felt the doings were lightweight and falsely melodramatic. Powell managed to demonstrate his acting skills in an unsympathetic role, however, and though what he did here was hardly calculated to set feminine hearts aflutter from Maine to California, he again demonstrated his range of characterization and his capacity for the projection of intense feeling.

Reed in an interview analyzed Powell's technique as "cerebral rather than emotional or instinctual. He has it all down in his mind, before he steps into the role; he has thought it all through, and most thoroughly, and that is why his characters ring true, no matter what melodramatic doings they are required to figure in."

Powell doesn't seem to be too popular with Ricardo Cortez; that's Estelle Taylor in 1927-style finerie. *(New York)*

LOVE'S GREATEST MISTAKE

1927 PARAMOUNT

Powell gives Josephine Dunn a hard time. (*Love's Greatest Mistake*)

CAST:

Evelyn Brent (*Jane*); William Powell (*Don Kendall*); James Hall (*Harvey Gibbs*); Josephine Dunn (*Honey McNeil*); Frank Morgan (*William Ogden*); Iris Gray (*Sara Foote*); Betty Byrne (*Lovey Gibbs*).

CREDITS:

Edward Sutherland (Director); Adolph Zukor, Jesse L. Lasky (Producers); William LeBaron (Associate Producer); Becky Gardiner (Scenario); based on *Love's Greatest Mistake* by Frederic Arnold Kummer; Leo Tover (Photographer).

Running time, 6 reels. Released February 1927.

ESSAY

In *Love's Greatest Mistake*, Powell was back in his usual rut as the Cad You Love to Hate. This time he brutally beats up Josephine Dunn because she refuses to give him financier Frank Morgan's love letters, with which Powell plans to do a fancy blackmailing job on Morgan. Soon Dunn's sister, Evelyn Brent, leaves her husband to run away with Powell, with Dunn finding eventual happiness with architect James Hall.

In the midst of these confused romantic doings, as directed by the competent Eddie Sutherland and written by Becky Gardiner, the public had a difficult time deciding on Powell as Consummate Cad or Perverse Inspirer of Sighs from the Ladies, and decided that he could—and must—be both. Handsome James Hall, ostensibly the "good guy" of the piece, showed himself no acting match for Powell's oily rascalities.

Will Powell get Evelyn Brent to make the right decision? (*Love's Greatest Mistake*)

Photoplay's reviewer stated that *Love's Greatest Mistake* "[delved] into the more hectic side of New York life," later adding, "[It's] brisk melodrama and good comedy."

Other reviewers wondered in print why Powell's blackmailing iniquities should be rewarded with the favors of comely Evelyn Brent, as the married woman who ran off with him, with one scribe deciding: "Perhaps they deserved each other."

Evelyn Brent was a dark-haired beauty with a somewhat glum and sinister aura which she employed to good effect in gangster films and other low-life cinematic ambiences. She and Powell were to meet again for more films, in which their respective chemistries matched well, her rueful cynicism dovetailing with his polished malfeasances.

An English reviewer, confronted with *Love's Greatest Mistake,* gave it as his opinion that "Mr. Powell is an attractive performer who seems to be cast as a bounder supreme in so many of his filmic incarnations. The wonder is that he makes his iniquities so attractive that they make the hero look pale and uninteresting. And that is no mean attainment."

SENORITA

1927 PARAMOUNT

CAST:

Bebe Daniels *(Senorita Francesca Hernandez);* James Hall *(Roger Oliveros);* William Powell *(Ramon Oliveros);* Josef Swickard *(Don Francisco Hernandez).*

CREDITS

Clarence Badger (Director); Adolph Zukor, Jesse L. Lasky (Producers); B. P. Schulberg (Associate Producer); John McDermott (Original Story); John McDermott, Lloyd Corrigan (Screenplay); H. Kinley Martin, William Marshall (Photographers).

Running time, 7 reels. Released April 1927.

Powell and Bebe Daniels, in male attire, duel it out. *(Senorita)*

What has female-clad (for a change) Daniels said to dumbfound Powell? *(Senorita)*

ESSAY

Photoplay informed its readers that in an item called *Senorita* "Bebe Daniels does a Fairbanks-Barrymore-Gilbert acrobatic stunt," adding, "This is her best picture in years. Highly recommended."

Somewhat ahead of its time in theme and content, *Senorita* displayed Daniels as a mannish swashbuckler, adept at shooting, fencing and breaking horses, who disguises her essential femininity because of family responsibilities. Her grandfather, owner of a ranch in South America (the family is native to the territory) summons his distant grandchild to

Powell and Daniels go in for a moustache-twirling contest. (*Senorita*)

It's hard to tell who's ahead in this particular scuffle. (*Senorita*)

The "Fairbanks-Gilbert-Barrymore" stunt that *Photoplay* praised. (*Senorita*)

aid him against his rivals, the Oliveroses. All this time, for reasons never too thoroughly explicated in the plot, he has believed her to be a man. Well, man she isn't, but as vividly portrayed by Daniels, she can do anything a man can, and fights with the best of them.

Powell appears as Ramon Oliveros, rival to the Hernandez family of Daniels and her grandfather, and soon he and the woman-disguised-as-caballero are fighting duels and raising assorted hell around the pampas. From Europe comes handsome James Hall, an Oliveros who is at first blind to Powell's depredations and destructivenesses, and he, too, is enlisted against Caballero Daniels, who has meanwhile restored the Hernandezes to prosperity and power.

Of course, Hall does not recognize that the girl he courts in feminine costume is also the caballero he must fight, and it is not until he wounds her during an attack on her ranch that he realizes the truth. After that the lovers follow nature's course, and the villainous Powell is given his just deserts.

Powell and Daniels always played well together, and they are in good form here, though it seems highly doubtful that he would not recognize her in her "male" disguises, which are flimsy at best and feature a fake moustache, a headband that looks more feminine than masculine and a pert bosom not too well disguised. But reality took second place to derring-do in *Senorita*.

SPECIAL DELIVERY

1927 PARAMOUNT

CAST:

Eddie Cantor (*Eddie, The Mail Carrier*); Jobyna Ralston (*Madge, The Girl*); William Powell (*Harold Jones, a Get-Rich-Quick Artist*); Donald Keith (*Harrigan, The Fireman*); Jack Dougherty (*Flannigan, a cop*); Victor Potel (*Nip, a detective*); Paul Kelly (*Tuck, another detective*); Mary Carr (*The Mother*).

Slinky, sinister Powell seeks to possess hapless Jobyna Ralston. *(Special Delivery)*

CREDITS:

William Goodrich (Director); Adolph Zukor, Jesse L. Lasky (Producers); B. P. Schulberg (Associate Producer); Eddie Cantor (Original Story); John Goodrich (Scenario and Adaptation); George Marion, Jr. (Titles); Henry Hallenberger (Photographer).

Running time, 6 reels. Released May 1927.

ESSAY

Powell supported Eddie Cantor in one of his few silent pictures, *Special Delivery*, playing a "get-rich-quick artist." Cantor, who had won great fame in the Ziegfeld Follies, had debuted before the cameras the year before, 1926, in *Kid Boots*, but he was to achieve his greatest fame as a comic in the talkies.

Here he is a buffoonish mail carrier in love with waitress Jobyna Ralston, who is also the object of admiration of fireman Donald Keith and cop Jack Dougherty. William Goodrich (the name Fatty Arbuckle took after a scandal ruined his career as a comic in films) directed this for fast chuckles and speedy action, with the histrionics kept to a minimum, at least among the stars. Powell is the villain of the piece yet again, and he has designs on Ralston which her other suitors seek to foil.

Powell manages to get Ralston to a ball where Eddie, who does not dance, seems to be on the sidelines, but during a black-bottom contest, in the film's most amusing and lively scene, he accidentally gets a piece of ice down his collar and proceeds in his panic and discomfort to gyrate so wildly that he wins the contest hands-down. Not that this does him any immediate good, for the manipulative and scheming Powell has managed to win Ralston as his fiancée. Of course all ends with the worm turning and Eddie exposing Powell as a swindler, thus winning Ralston.

Goodrich-Arbuckle, given his years of experience as a before-the-camera comic in early silents, managed to guide Cantor skillfully through his second silent, and the comedian made a good impression on 1927 audiences, without, however, achieving the major impact that he would make after sound came to the movies. Powell is nefariously smooth as ever, and, despite his villainous aura, projects the slimy sex appeal that an innocent girl would find magnetic—until. . . . *Photoplay*'s verdict: "Eddie Cantor and a lot of gags, some new and some not so new," adding, "but a snappy evening."

TIME TO LOVE

1927 PARAMOUNT

Powell and Griffith prepare for a duel, to Vera Veronina's consternation. (*Time to Love*)

CAST:

Raymond Griffith (*Alfred Sava-Goiu*); William Powell (*Prince Alado*); Vera Veronina (*Countess Elvire*); Josef Swickard (*Elvire's Father*); Mario Carillo (*First Duellist*); Pierre De Ramey (*Second Duellist*); Helene Giere (*Elvire's Guardian*); Alfred Sabato (*Hindu Mystic*).

CREDITS:

Frank Tuttle (Director); Adolph Zukor, Jesse L. Lasky (Producers); B. P. Schulberg (Associate Producer); Alfred Savoir (Original Story); Pierre Collings (Screenplay); William Marshall (Photographer).

Running time, 5 reels. Released June 1927.

74

ESSAY

A fast-paced farce directed by Frank Tuttle, *Time to Love* had Powell yet again as the wrong corner in the triangle, the other two being Raymond Griffith, the star, and Vera Veronina. After a romantic disappointment, Griffith attempts suicide but lands instead in the boat of a countess, Veronina, whose boat happens to pass just under him as he leaps.

Though love develops for Griffith, it turns out that Veronina, via the will of her imperious father, Josef Swickard, is engaged to Prince Alado (Powell). Imagining that Veronina loves Powell, Griffith challenges him to a duel, but pretends he has been killed in it and goes to America, even after the lady has told him she prefers him to Powell.

Changing his mind again, Griffith returns and snatches Veronina from her wedding. They escape in a balloon, get pulled through a train tunnel, then parachute back to Countess Elvire's castle. The minister, not knowing there has been a change of grooms due to his nearsightedness, thereupon marries them with dispatch. As for the unlucky Powell, he is dispatched to the limbo to which all good (rather, all bad) movie villains go.

Raymond Griffith had a flourishing career as a comedy lead in the silents, but his starring career ended with the coming of sound; after that, he became a producer for Fox Films. He is best remembered today for his only memorable sound appearance, as the dying soldier in *All Quiet on the Western Front*. As for Vera Veronina, she turned out to be a flash in the silent pan of which little or nothing was heard thereafter.

Photoplay thought little of *Time To Love*, with its reviewer sniffing: "Raymond Griffith trying to prove how silly he can be—and proving it, too. Of course, if you have a lot of time to waste. . . ."

There was some praise by other critics of the balloon and tunnel effects, and director Tuttle kept the action percolating, but *Time to Love* was strictly an also-ran that did nothing for Powell.

PAID TO LOVE

1927 FOX

CAST:

George O'Brien *(Crown Prince Michael);* Virginia Valli *(Gaby);* J. Farrell MacDonald *(Peter Roberts);* Thomas Jefferson *(King);* William Powell *(Prince Eric);* Merta Sterling *(Maid);* Hank Mann *(Servant).*

CREDITS

Howard Hawks (Director); William Fox (Producer); Harry Carr (Original Story); William M. Conselman, Seton I. Miller (Scenario); Benjamin Glazer (Adaptation); William O'Connell (Photographer).

Running time, 7 reels. Released July 1927.

ESSAY

Director Howard Hawks, of whom much was to be heard in the 1930's and 1940's, won *Photoplay*'s approval for his tongue-in-cheek direction of a spoof on Balkan kingdoms and their unrealistic romancings in the sparkling *Paid to Love.* The magazine's reviewer called it "a sprightly, charmingly directed comedy that kids the old hokum of a mythical kingdom romance."

Here Powell had little to do but strut about in a snappy white uniform with polished boots and buckle; his is a subsidiary character, and up front is the romancing of George O'Brien as Crown Prince Michael, of yet another Ruritanian kingdom, and Virginia Valli as a girl from an apache cafe who is drafted as O'Brien's fiancée by American banker J. Farrell MacDonald, who feels the prince should be getting married. Since Valli and O'Brien have fallen in love, the unsuitability of their alliance is (in this film, anyway) remedied by

Powell inspects Virginia Valli's charms while disengaging his spur from her dress. *(Paid to Love)*

J. Farrell MacDonald meets O'Brien as Powell attends. *(Paid to Love)*

Powell gives his attention to the servant girl while O'Brien gets the cap. *(Paid to Love)*

making her a duchess and indoctrinating her in court ways. Of course the Seton I. Miller–William M. Conselman screenplay, based on an original story by Harry Carr, was totally outlandish in every respect, farce and merciless kidding of the Ruritanian convention being the aims.

Particularly amusing was the sight of George O'Brien, a movie hero who was far more at home on a horse in a Western, uncomfortable as the crown prince of a Balkan kingdom. You didn't believe him for a minute, nor the situations that surrounded him, nor Virginia Valli's transformation, in about ten minutes, from cafe girl to duchess. Most at home, combining farce with a fair amount of scintillation, was Powell, who got into the spirit of things as dashing Prince Eric with éclat. The role, however, was too reminiscent of too many he had already essayed, despite his efforts to freshen it up, and didn't really advance his stock. However, he did, as some women's-mag reviewers noted, look quite handsome and dashing in his uniforms.

Powell has a dressing-table discussion with Virginia Valli. *(Paid to Love)*

NEVADA

1927 PARAMOUNT

CAST:

Gary Cooper *(Nevada);* Thelma Todd *(Hettie Ide);* William Powell *(Clan Dillon);* Philip Strange *(Ben Ide);* Ernie S. Adams *(Cash Burridge);* Christian J. Frank *(Sheriff of Winthrop);* Ivan Christy *(Cawthorne);* Guy Oliver *(Sheriff of Lineville).*

CREDITS:

John Waters (Director); Adolph Zukor, Jesse L. Lasky (Producers); John Stone, L. G. Rigby (Screenplay); based on the novel by Zane Grey; C. Edgar Schoenbaum (Photographer).

Running time, 7 reels. Released August 1927.

ESSAY

Powell found himself the bad guy in *Nevada,* a full-blown shoot-em-up Western star-ring Gary Cooper, at 26 already a Western hero. Cooper is on the side of right and chief romancer to the girl in question, in this case Thelma Todd, who is surprisingly fresh and naïve in this, considering her later hard-boiled and comical incarnations in comedies and melodramas of the 1930's.

Based on a Zane Grey novel and directed by John Waters in a fast-moving, tough-spirited style, *Nevada* was styled by *Photoplay* "a de luxe western, with . . . beautiful scenery, fine acting and plenty of thrills." In wide black hat, string tie and black outfit, Powell is a sinister and magnetic bad man indeed, every bit a match for virile and virtuous Cooper. In the climactic confrontation, Powell even wounds Cooper, but our hero is saved by the arrival of a posse with evidence convicting Powell of all manner of malfeasances.

Powell and Cooper are also rivals for the hand of Thelma Todd. It seems that her father has drafted the intrepid Cooper to protect her from cattle rustlers who threaten his property. Powell, ostensibly the ranch foreman, is in reality the leader of the rustlers, and covets Todd; he is determined, as the titles of silent Westerns would have it, "to possess her at all costs." A lot of people get

Bad-guy Powell covets Thelma Todd, but she's having none of it. *(Nevada)*

killed before the final Cooper-Powell confrontation, and it's all stylishly exciting and "a Western from a worthy tradition," as another reviewer put it.

In this Powell proves that he can ride a horse and rough it up with the best of them, and his eyes glitter and his posturings menace in the best tradition of classic Western bad men. In fact, so attractive is he that one wonders why Todd doesn't fancy his complex negativisms over Cooper's rather dull and Rinsowhite positives, but 1927 movie-Western conventions dictated that Cooper win the heroine for his very own. As for Powell, it's off to the clink.

SHE'S A SHEIK

1927 PARAMOUNT

Daniels makes it plain she will have none of Powell. *(She's a Sheik)*

CAST:

Bebe Daniels *(Zaida)*; Richard Arlen *(Captain Colton)*; William Powell *(Kada)*; Josephine Dunn *(Wanda Fowler)*; James Bradbury, Jr. *(Jerry)*; Billy Franey *(Joe)*; Paul McAllister *(Sheik Yusif Ben Hamad)*; Al Fremont *(The Major)*.

CREDITS:

Clarence Badger (Director); Adolph Zukor, Jesse L. Lasky (Producers); Lloyd Corrigan, Grover

Daniels's rapier has put Powell in his place. *(She's a Sheik)*

Jones (Screenplay); John McDermott (Original Story); George Marion, Jr. (Titles); J. Roy Hunt (Photographer).

Running time, 6 reels. Released November 1927

ESSAY

Bebe Daniels and William Powell seemed to have a special chemistry together, if late twenties fan reaction was any indication, and again they found themselves cast together in one of those adventure films in which Daniels specialized at the time. But as usual, Powell was not the hero; in fact he got third billing, behind Daniels and handsome Richard Arlen, who for a time threatened to rival Gary Cooper in this type of role.

Arlen is the object of Daniels's desire, but her more colorful and adventurous scenes are played with Powell. Again Daniels adopts masculine garb and does the swashbuckling that amused audiences in *Senorita* earlier in the year. She is the granddaughter of a sheik (Paul McAllister) who, because she is half-

Powell and swashbuckling Daniels go at it for real. *(She's a Sheik)*

Daniels scorns the flower-toting Powell. *(She's A Sheik)*

Watch out, Daniels is ready for you! *(She's a Sheik)*

Spanish as well as half-Arabian, has made up her mind that she will have none but a Christian husband. Enter Powell as Kada, a bad man of the desert this time, who is determined to have her as his own, whether she likes it or not. Hence the duelling and rapiering which for a time keeps the importu-

79

nate Powell, sinister indeed in dark makeup, at bay.

Meanwhile, as the ubiquitous, energetic and highly sexed Zaida, Daniels encounters handsome Captain Colton (Arlen) whose manly charms arouse her, and she boldly kidnaps him to her desert lair (as is obvious, there is more than a little borrowing, all in tongue-in-cheek terms, from Valentino's final film, *The Son of the Sheik* [1926], with the sexes reversed). Meanwhile Powell isn't letting her get away, and he and his men go on the attack. Under Clarence Badger's direction, there is a lively finale, with two friends of Daniels, American showmen Billy Franey and James Bradbury, Jr., projecting a film that purports to show attacking warriors; this frightens off the ignorant tribesmen, who know nothing of movies and think it's the real thing.

Admiring fans of both Daniels and Powell began writing in asking why they didn't appear opposite each other as romantic leads. Arlen, handsome as he was, seems to have come off third best in this film, at least with the public.

THE LAST COMMAND

1928 PARAMOUNT

CAST:

Emil Jannings *(General Dolgoruki/Grand Duke Sergius Alexander)*; William Powell *(Leo Andreiev)*; Evelyn Brent *(Natasha Dobrowa)*; Nicholas Soussanin *(Adjutant)*; Michael Visaroff *(Serge, the Valet)*; Jack Raymond *(Assistant Director)*; Viacheslav Savitsky *(a Pirate)*; Fritz Feld *(a Revolutionist)*; Harry Semels *(Soldier Extra)*; Alexander Ikonnikov, Nicholas Kobyliansky *(Drillmasters)*.

CREDITS:

Josef Von Sternberg (Director); Adolph Zukor, Jesse L. Lasky (Producers); B. P. Schulberg (Associate Producer); J. G. Bachmann (Supervisor); John F. Goodrich (Adapter, Screenplay); Lajos

Brent watches as revolutionist Powell confers with a soldier. *(The Last Command)*

Biro (Original Story); Herman J. Mankiewicz (Titles); Bert Glennon (Photographer); Hans Dreier (Set Designer); Fred C. Ryle (Makeup); Nicholas Kobyliansky (Technical Director); William Shea (Editor).

Running time, 9 reels. Released January 1928.

ESSAY

The Last Command gave Powell one of his best parts up to that time, and he found himself, to his gratification, in a major picture opposite a top star, the brilliant German actor Emil Jannings, who was to win one of the first Oscars for his role of a Russian general reduced to humiliating status as a Hollywood extra.

Powell plays Leo Andreiev, once a Russian revolutionist, now an established movie director. In a flashback, it is shown that Jannings had paraded pompously as a Russian grand duke and general in the Czarist days in Russia. Oppressive to the lower classes, he had once abused Powell with his whip. In love with a spy, Evelyn Brent, Jannings is brutally beaten by the revolutionary mob and becomes palsied when he sees the wrecking of a train carrying his beloved.

In Hollywood, ten years later, Jannings is a pitiful figure indeed, unable to keep up with the younger, stronger extras who try to edge him out in the struggle for his only livelihood. Actuated by a bitter irony, Powell enlists the old man in a scene for his new picture, in which he is to face off some rebelling soldiers; once again he is to be the Czarist general facing the troops, but the strain is too much for him and he dies.

The original title had been *The General,* and it was written as an original screenplay by director Josef Von Sternberg, based on an idea the great Ernst Lubitsch himself had

given him. Von Sternberg proved a masterly director in this, guiding Jannings, whose temperament and mystique he well understood, to the heights of his silent career. Jannings's

Brent and Powell are at Jannings's mercy in this flashback scene. *(The Last Command)*

Powell, Brent and the Russian soldier in a confrontation. *(The Last Command)*

81

German accent, thick and heavy, was to doom him in America at the coming of the talkies, but he and Von Sternberg would be triumphantly reunited for *The Blue Angel* in Germany the following year (a talkie version, too).

Powell is excellent as the ironically sadistic director, who hates Jannings not only because of his Czarist past but because he was his rival for Brent. The two actors play off each other beautifully in the heartrending final scene, all the stronger because Sternberg emphasized, throughout, fateful irony rather than sentiment.

(who had fourth billing) the likes of Evelyn Brent, Noah Beery and Roscoe Karns.

Powell as usual was the dastardly villain, this time named Becque, who vied with Cooper throughout a running time which involved much hurrying about in the sands of the Sahara desert, assorted plots, and duels and fights galore. Winning the title "Beau Sabreur" for his duelling success, Cooper goes to talk a sheik into an important treaty but is foiled by Powell, who leads an attack. After more skirmishes comes a climactic duel in which Cooper kills Powell.

BEAU SABREUR

1928 PARAMOUNT

CAST:

Gary Cooper *(Major Henri de Beaujolais);* Evelyn Brent *(Mary Van Brugh);* William Powell *(Becque);* Noah Beery *(Sheik El Hammel);* Roscoe Karns *(Buddy);* Mitchell Lewis *(Suleman the Strong);* Arnold Kent *(Raoul de Redon);* Raoul Paoli *(Dufour);* Joan Standing *(Maudie);* Frank Reicher *(General de Beaujolais);* Oscar Smith *(Djikki).*

CREDITS:

John Waters (Director); Adolph Zukor, Jesse L. Lasky (Producers); Tom J. Geraghty (Scenario and Adaptation); based on *Beau Sabreur* by Percival Christopher Wren; Julian Johnson (Titles); C. Edgar Schoenbaum (Photographer); Rose Lowenger (Editor).

Running time, 7 reels. Released January 1928.

ESSAY

Again Gary Cooper and Powell were in a picture together, this one an attempt via a similar title to repeat the success of the 1926 *Beau Geste.* Originating from the pen of Percival Christopher Wren, who had written *Beau Geste,* this effort was directed by John Waters, and featured, along with Cooper and Powell

Powell in an outfit that must have set new style trends in North Africa. *(Beau Sabreur)*

Powell and Noah Beery chew the fat. *(Beau Sabreur)*

Powell is done up in some ambitious Arabian outfits, and his turbans and cloaks and caftans must have set new style trends when the picture was shown in North Africa. Evelyn Brent, the leading woman, was to figure with Powell in subsequent, and more important, films.

Photoplay opined: "Not another *Beau Geste* but a thrilling and picturesque tale nonetheless. You'll like Evelyn Brent, Gary Cooper, William Powell and Noah Beery." Other reviewers questioned why Powell seemed doomed to perpetual exotic-villain roles, and his friend Ronald Colman counseled him to avoid these roles if at all possible. But Powell was under contract to Paramount, and his star-clout was still to come, and he had to accept roles that the studio overlords deemed appropriate to his looks and manner—at least as they conceived of them.

Some film commentators of the period expressed the hope that the "Beau" pictures would not become an endless cycle, the material being of the kind that could inevitably lose its freshness if overplayed. Some felt it had *long since* been overplayed in one form or another.

FEEL MY PULSE

1928 PARAMOUNT

CAST:

Bebe Daniels *(Barbara Manning);* Richard Arlen *(Her Problem);* William Powell *(Her Nemesis);* Melbourne MacDowell *(Her Uncle Wilberforce);* George Irving *(Her Uncle Edgar);* Charles Sellon *(Her Sanitarium's Caretaker);* Heinie Conklin *(Her Patient).*

CREDITS:

Gregory La Cava (Director); Adolph Zukor, Jesse L. Lasky (Producers); Howard Emmett Rogers (Original Story); Keene Thompson, Nick Barrows (Scenario); George Marion, Jr. (Titles); J. Roy Hunt (Photographer); E. Lloyd Sheldon (Editor).

Running time, 6 reels. Released February 1928.

ESSAY

Bebe Daniels was starred in *Feel My Pulse,* and again Richard Arlen, cast as her romantic

At first Daniels is taken in by the "sanitarium" look of Powell's layout. *(Feel My Pulse)*

Powell cues Daniels in on the uses of guns. *(Feel My Pulse)*

interest, won her in the end; fans' letters urging that she be co-starred with William Powell continued to be ignored. This time Daniels, who since childhood had been driven into hypochondria by the mistaken belief that she is sickly, goes off to an island sanitarium where a gang of rum-runners, headed by Powell, are posing as patients in order to carry on their nefarious activities. Disguised as one of them is a reporter, Richard Arlen, who proposes to write the truth about them.

When the gang go after Arlen, Daniels, who has responded to his declaration of love, realizes she is not so sick after all, and fends them off with whatever comes to hand, including chloroform and surgical instruments. Powell goes on a menacing rampage with firearms and what-not, but is foiled by the Arlen-Daniels combine. Realizing, now, that she is perfectly healthy after all her derring-do activities, Daniels, looks forward to happiness with Arlen.

Once again, Powell was relegated to limbo as the dastardly villain; by now he had become

Powell menaces Daniels and her light o' love Arlen.
(Feel My Pulse)

Powell plays innocent while Daniels waxes suspicious. *(Feel My Pulse)*

somewhat resigned to such casting. "It's that raised-eyebrow, infinitely sardonic look you have," the director Gregory La Cava told him. "When villains are cast, you are the first one to come to mind." But La Cava was one of the

first to predict Powell's coming eminence in romantic comedy lead roles, and in fact was one day to direct him in one of the best, *My Man Godfrey*. But that, of course, was some eight years in the future.

La Cava, who had had a variegated early career, had begun directing feature films as early as 1922; his sharp comic sense was quickly noticed, but it took the Thirties and the Talkie Era to bring him fully into his own. *Photoplay* noted with a sniff: "Bebe Daniels is terribly annoyed by William Powell and his rum gang. Fairly good, but not up to Bebe's standard."

PARTNERS IN CRIME

1928 PARAMOUNT

CAST:

Wallace Beery *(Mike Doolan, The Detective);* Raymond Hatton *("Scoop" McGee, The Reporter);* Mary Brian *(Marie Burke, The Cigarette Girl);* William Powell *(Smith);* Jack Luden *(Richard Deming, Assistant District Attorney);* Arthur Housman *(Barton);* Albert Roccardi *(Kanelli, The Restaurant Owner);* Joseph W. Girard *(Chief of Police);* George Irving *(B. B. Cornwall);* Bruce Gordon *(Dodo);* Jack Richardson *(Jake).*

CREDITS:

Frank Strayer (Director); Adolph Zukor, Jesse L. Lasky (Producer); Grover Jones, Gilbert Pratt (Story and Screenplay); George Marion Jr. (Titles); William Marshall (Photographer); William Shea (Editor).

Running time, 7 reels. Released March 1928.

ESSAY

Photoplay dismissed Powell's next, in which again he was the eternal villain, in few words: "Beery and Hatton in the underworld. Mostly gags. You know the type." Raymond Hatton, as a reporter, and Wallace Beery, as a detective, dominated the action here, with Powell in a thankless, strictly subsidiary role as one Smith, who does the usual menacing. Most of the action is taken up with the efforts of Beery and Hatton to save Jack Luden, an innocent suspect in a store robbery, at the urging of Mary Brian, his sweetheart. Enamored of the girl, the two clowns find themselves enmeshed in an all-out gang war, and in their assorted bumblings, set off, accidentally, some police tear-gas bombs. Brian eventually summons the police, who rescue her lover.

Along for the ride in all this was Powell, who attempts to seduce Brian and performs other acts of skullduggery. He could have phoned in his performance, had the movies been talking yet, but as it was, he managed to make an impression in an unimpressive role, and if (as yet) one couldn't hear him, one could savor his visual impact.

Beery and Hatton hogged the footage in this, via their mugging and hilarious overacting. The story, directed by Frank Strayer,

Powell playfully tries to outmug Beery in this scene. *(Partners in Crime)*

from a screenplay by Grover Jones and Gilbert Pratt, veered uneasily between farce (courtesy of the Beery-Hatton combine) and melodrama of the more obvious and awkward kind. Result: no one, even Powell, emerged from this farrago with any advancement of his/her career. Mary Brian, who was to go on to some prominence, of a limited kind, in later pictures, was a sweet-faced heroine of earnest mien who found herself lost in this; little was heard, in the future, of director Frank Strayer.

Powell later cited the film as an example of the nonsense into which he was forced in the days before he had developed a contractual clout at Paramount. Shortly his already conceded visual appeal would be enhanced by his resonant, stage-trained voice.

Hatton and Beery look on as Powell tries to seduce Brian. *(Partners in Crime)*

THE DRAGNET

1928 PARAMOUNT

CAST:

George Bancroft *(Two-Gun Nolan);* William Powell *(Dapper Frank Trent);* Evelyn Brent *(The Magpie);* Fred Kohler *("Gabby" Steve);* Francis McDonald *(Sniper Dawson);* Leslie Fenton *(Shakespeare).*

Powell ponders his next crime. *(The Dragnet)*

Powell and Evelyn Brent have a tense drink. *(The Dragnet)*

Powell and Brent seem bored with each other. *(The Dragnet)*

CREDITS:

Josef Von Sternberg (Director); Oliver H. P. Garrett (Original Story); Jules Furthman, Charles Furthman (Scenario); Jules Furthman (Adaptation); Harold Rosson (Photographer); Hans Dreier (Set Designer); Helen Lewis (Editor).

Running time, 8 reels. Released May 1928.

ESSAY

Photoplay went all-out for the Josef Von Sternberg-directed *The Dragnet*, with its reviewer raving: "Vivid and swiftly moving underworld story with Grade-A acting by George Bancroft, William Powell and Evelyn Brent." While *The Dragnet* was not in the class of Von Sternberg's earlier, brilliant *Underworld*, it was indeed a creditable film, and this time, in yet another villain role ("a slimy crime lord," one magazine reviewer called him), Powell, under the Von Sternberg guidance, managed to turn in a performance glowing with sinister force of a charismatic kind that established his acting credentials as never before, except perhaps in *The Last Command*.

The lively Jules and Charles Furthman screenplay from an original story by Oliver H. P. Garrett also drew star performances from George Bancroft and Evelyn Brent. Bancroft is a hardboiled police detective with an alcoholic bent, named Two-Gun Nolan. During a battle with a gang, his partner, Leslie Fenton, was killed, and he mistakenly believes that he fired the fatal bullet. The gang was led by Powell, known as "Dapper Frank Trent," a charmer and fancy dresser who conceals a killer's heart under his polished exterior.

In despair, and sinking into alcoholism, Bancroft is informed by Evelyn Brent that it was actually Powell who killed his buddy, thus reviving Bancroft from his despairing stupor and motivating him toward revenge. When Powell, who is involved with Brent after a fashion, learns of her duplicity, he shoots and wounds her, then is killed by Bancroft. Bancroft then returns to police duty and makes Brent (known throughout the film as "The Magpie") his wife.

A Von Sternberg picture always meant interesting visual and atmospheric touches (he was one of the few directors whose style in that and later periods was unmistakable), and here he took a crime drama that in other hands might have been pedestrian and transformed it into something vivid and individualistic. While not first-rate Von Sternberg, it is one of his more creditable efforts nonetheless.

THE VANISHING PIONEER

1928 PARAMOUNT

CAST:

Jack Holt (*Anthony Ballard/John Ballard*); Sally Blane (*June Shelby*); William Powell (*John Murdock*); Fred Kohler (*Sheriff Murdock*); Guy Oliver (*Mr. Shelby*); Roscoe Karns (*Ray Hearn*); Tim Holt (*John Ballard, Age 7*); Marcia Manon (*The Apron Woman*).

CREDITS:

John Waters (Director); J. Walter Ruben (Scenario); from a story by Zane Grey; John Goodrich, Ray Harris (Adaptation); G. Edgar Schoenbaum (Photographer); Doris Drought (Editor).

Running time, 6 reels. Released June 1928.

Holt and Powell take each other's measure as Sally Blane minds her business. (*The Vanishing Pioneer*)

Powell got short shrift in a *Photoplay* review of *The Vanishing Pioneer.* "The return of Jack Holt to the Paramount ranch. And the result is a Grade A Western," its reviewer said. In this forgettable Western, fine in its time, Holt leads some pioneer settlers who are threatened with a loss of water supply because the nearby townspeople want to be rid of them. Corrupt local politico Powell and his brother (Fred Kohler, regarded at the time as "the perfect villain" in film circles) intend to acquire all water rights, and will not hesitate to use the most nefarious methods to accomplish their goals.

Of course, pretty Sally Blane is on hand to repulse the villains and cheer on the hero. Powell frames Holt with a murder rap, Holt must flee temporarily, but later returns, gets Powell to admit to the murder, and, after Powell attempts to escape, shoots him. The pioneers win back their water access, and then are persuaded that the town's needs supersede theirs. Paid for the land, the pioneers keep moving westward via covered wagon.

Again Powell was saddled with a stock villain role, getting neither his objectives *nor* the girl, and this time around reviewers across the country wrote reviews mentioning the waste of Powell's talents in language that amounted to: "Hold! Enough!"

One Chicago critic wrote: "Mr. Powell was born to be a star, and a star he will be, sooner or later, despite the trash in which he is consistently drowned, and while *The Vanishing Pioneer* displays the likes of Jack Holt in a setting right for him, it constitutes a scandalous waste of the Powell talents to keep him subjected to repetitious roles like this—repetitious in the sense that he has done variations on mountebanks of this kind for much too long, and in too many pictures. When is Paramount going to see the light, and cast him with more variety?"

Powell in an uncharacteristic pose. *(Forgotten Faces)*

FORGOTTEN FACES

1928 PARAMOUNT

CAST:

Clive Brook *(Heliotrope Harry Harlow);* Mary Brian *(Alice Deane);* William Powell *(Froggy);* Baclanova *(Lilly Harlow);* Fred Kohler *(Number 1309);* Jack Luden *(Tom).*

CREDITS:

Victor Schertzinger (Director); Howard Estabrook (Scenario); Oliver H. P. Garrett (Adaptation); based on a magazine story by Richard Washburn Child; Julian Johnson (Titles); J. Roy Hunt (Photographer); David Selznick, George Nichols, Jr. (Editors); David Selznick (Supervisor).

Running time, 8 reels. Released August 1928.

ESSAY

"Underworld story of regeneration and sacrifice. Fine story, fine acting and 100 percent entertainment" *Photoplay* said of *Forgotten*

Powell lays down the law. *(Forgotten Faces)*

Faces. The story had such perennial appeal that it got made over and over, getting filmed in 1920, 1928, 1936, and, finally, as *A Gentleman After Dark,* with Brian Donlevy, in 1942. The 1928 version is considered the best. Written by Howard Estabrook from the story "A Whiff of Heliotrope" by Richard Washburn Child, and sensitively directed by Victor Schertzinger, the story dealt with one Heliotrope Harry Harlow (Clive Brook), who, upon finding out that his wife is unfaithful, murders her lover. Before surrendering, Brook leaves his daughter at the doorstep of a well-to-do couple who proceed to raise her as their own.

Fifteen years pass. Brook's wife, Olga Baclanova, discovers the child's whereabouts after a long search and threatens to reclaim her daughter, despite the protests of Brook, who is still in prison. Released on parole, Brook obtains a post as butler in the home

Seated on a park bench, Powell and Brook look grim. *(Forgotten Faces)*

where his daughter has been harbored, and prevents her mother from seeing her. Finally, to protect his daughter, he deliberately provokes Baclanova into killing him; the mother in turn is sent to prison, and the daughter, at last, is safe from future harm.

In 1928 the outrageous sentimentalities implicit in this situation and the forced situations and coincidences were ignored in the interest of the human values of the story, a 1928 example of total "suspension of disbelief." By the time the Donlevy version was made in 1942, with aspects of the plot altered, the old-fashioned, maudlin nature of the tale had become obvious. But in 1928 the good acting helped put over the story.

And where was Powell in all this? He played a sleazy subsidiary character named Froggie who dallies with Baclanova and is otherwise up to no good. Some fans wrote that he would have been more suited for the lead than Brook, having more expressiveness as an actor, but sleazy he was destined to be in *Forgotten Faces*. But he did put vividness and bite into his role.

INTERFERENCE

1928 PARAMOUNT

CAST:

William Powell *(Philip Voaze)*; Evelyn Brent *(Deborah Kane)*; Clive Brook *(Sir John Marlay)*; Doris Kenyon *(Faith Marlay)*; Tom Ricketts *(Charles Smith)*; Brandon Hurst *(Inspector Haynes)*; Louis Payne *(Childers)*; Wilfred Noy *(Dr. Gray)*; Donald Stuart *(Freddie)*; Raymon Lawrence *(Reporter)*.

CREDITS:

Lothar Mendes (Director, Silent Version); Roy J. Pomeroy (Director, Dialogue Scenes); Louise Long (Continuity); Ernest Pascal (Dialogue); Julian Johnson (Titles); Hope Loring (Adaptation); based on a play by Roland Pertwee and Harold Dearden; Henry Gerrard (Photographer); George Nichols, Jr. (Editor); Franklin Hansen (Chief Recording Engineer); Movietone Sound.

Running time, 10 reels (7 reels silent version). Released December 1928.

Powell and Brent don't dally romantically for long. *(Interference)*

Brent threatens Powell with blackmail. *(Interference)*

Doris Kenyon is torn between husbands present and past. *(Interference)*

ESSAY

Interference was the first picture in which audiences from Maine to California heard Powell's rich, melodious, utterly distinctive voice—a voice that, along with his fey, individualistic good looks, would take him into a whole new dimension of audience appeal, and on to major stardom.

Shot by Lothar Mendes in a silent version and by Roy Pomeroy in the talkie rendition, *Interference* in its latter version was historically significant, as it was Paramount's first all-out venture in the talkie medium. Thanks to Powell's compelling vocal presence and the fine performances around him, the picture had quite an impact, though the story was trite, and the necessary constrictions hampered the actors' movements (the sound technique forced, for the time, stationary mikes and rigid camera placements).

"A Grade A murder story—well acted and well spoken" was *Photoplay's* opinion in its December 1928 issue (the film got into circulation in time for Christmas of that year, and

With Powell and Brent, it's the quiet before the storm. *(Interference)*

inaugurated the talkie revolution of the following year, 1929), but other critics felt that Powell in his talkie debut had deserved a

93

fresher story. There was also some comment that being directed by two different people in the talkie and silent versions had caused a confusion of his style. But for the most part the public of late 1928 flocked to see a picture in which Powell spoke for the first time, and he was the true reason for its popularity.

The Movietone sound was, of course, a novelty, and Roy Pomeroy deserves credit for guiding the actors including Evelyn Brent and Doris Kenyon, both inexperienced with the new technique, so well. The story has Powell, reportedly killed in action in World War I, actually living in London in disguise. His wife, Doris Kenyon, thinking him dead, has remarried, and an old flame of Powell's, Brent, tries to blackmail her. Knowing he is dying of a heart condition, and determined to spare Kenyon from scandal, Powell kills Brent, and then turns himself in to the law.

According to critics cross-country, it was Powell's picture all the way.

THE CANARY MURDER CASE

1929 PARAMOUNT

CAST:

William Powell (*Philo Vance*); James Hall (*Jimmy Spotswoode*); Louise Brooks (*Margaret O'Dell*); Jean Arthur (*Alys La Fosse*); Gustav von Seyffertitz (*Dr. Ambrose Lindquist*); Charles Lane (*Charles Spotswoode*); Eugene Pallette (*Ernest Heath*); Lawrence Grant (*Charles Cleaver*); Ned Sparks (*Tony Skeel*); Louis John Bartels (*Louis Mannix*); E. H. Calvert (*Markham*); and George Y. Harvey, Oscar Smith, Tim Adair.

CREDITS

Malcolm St. Clair (Director); Florence Ryerson (Scenario/Adaptation); Albert S. Levino (Co-Adapter); Dialogue by S. S. Van Dine; based on his

story; Herman J. Mankiewicz (Titles); Harry Fischbeck (Photographer); William Shea (Editor); Movietone.

Running time, 7 reels. Released February 1929.

Co-star Brooks refused to dub for the talkie version. (*The Canary Murder Case*)

ESSAY

The Paramount executives, anxious to cash in on Powell's new popularity as a talkie star, rushed him next into *The Canary Murder Case*, based on one of S. S. Van Dine's popular mysteries. The role of Philo Vance suited Powell to a T. Vance was polished, worldly, suave, erudite and sharp-minded, the sophisticated detective supreme, and Powell made the most of the role, injecting, as he later said, more humanity and humor into the part than Van Dine had originally visualized. In defense of his changes, he said that Vance on the screen had to have more dimension and all around personality than was necessary in a book, where the literary approach and the mystery were more important. Van Dine him-

Powell clears the innocent James Hall. (*The Canary Murder Case*)

E.H. Calvert, Pallette and Powell, along with a cop, ponder the mystery.
(*The Canary Murder Case*)

Calvert, Powell and Pallette made an amusing investigatory team. *(The Canary Murder Case)*

self seemed to agree, for he commended Powell's performance.

Photoplay felt *The Canary Murder Case* was "logical and well-constructed" and that Powell was "perfectly swell" as the detective. A silent version had been shot by director Mal St. Clair in 1928; then it was decided to reshoot it extensively to capitalize on the talkie boom, with much new dialogue, some of it by Van Dine himself, added. Frank Tuttle ably directed the talkie version.

Louise Brooks had originally been cast opposite Powell in the silent version, but after she went to Germany to make films, she refused to return for the dubbing into talkie form. Margaret Livingston took over for Brooks in the talkie version, or at least her voice did. (Oddly enough, Brooks had a perfectly good voice for talkies, so her self-destructiveness is all the more tragic.) The story dealt with the murder of a Broadway musical star, known as "The Canary." It seems Brooks, who played the role, was up to some blackmailing shenanigans. Eugene Pallette appeared as the dumb police sergeant, and E. H. Calvert is the district attorney.

James Hall is at first wrongly accused, then the real murderer (we won't spoil it for viewers of the re-runs by telling his name) is exposed. The ingenious plotting sported all the usual Van Dine false alarms. It was his first novel to reach the screen.

Louise Brooks, as the Canary, is suspended high above the musical stage. *(The Canary Murder Case)*

THE FOUR FEATHERS

1929 PARAMOUNT

CAST:

Richard Arlen *(Harry Feversham);* Fay Wray *(Ethne Eustace);* Clive Brook *(Lieutenant Durrance);* William Powell *(Captain Trench);* Theodore Von Eltz *(Lieutenant Castleton);* Noah Beery *(Slave Trader);* Zack Williams *(Idris);* Noble Johnson *(Ahmed);* Harold Hightower *(Ali);* Philippe De Lacy *(Harry at 10);* E. J. Radcliffe *(Colonel Eustace);* George Fawcett *(Colonel Faversham);* Augustin Symonds *(Colonel Sutch).*

CREDITS:

Merian C. Cooper, Ernest B. Schoedsack, Lothar Mendes (Directors); David O. Selznick (Associate Producer); Howard Estabrook (Screenplay); based on *The Four Feathers* by Alfred Edward Woodley Mason; Julian Johnson, John Farrow (Titles); Hope Loring (Adaptation); Robert Kurrle, Merian C. Cooper, Ernest B. Schoedsack (Photographers); William Frederick Peters (Music); Ernest B. Schoedsack (Editor).

Running time, 8 reels. Released June 1929.

ESSAY

The Four Feathers was to be Powell's final silent film—meaning the last one in which his voice was not heard, for it was to be released in two versions, silent, and with sound and synchronized effects but no dialogue. Since 1929 was the year that the talkies dominated the terrain, it was an act of courage on the part of Paramount to release a picture that, since it was without dialogue, was already outdated.

The story, based on the novel *The Four Feathers* (1902) by Alfred Edward Woodley Mason, was to prove a popular one for over 50 years in the cinema, being made in 1921, 1939 and 1955, as well as in 1928, the Powell version, and as late as 1977.

Richard Arlen, in 1929 Paramount's most promising male lead, plays a British Army officer who resigns out of cowardice. He receives the white feather, a symbol of cowardice, from his three former Army comrades,

Von Eltz, Powell and Brook get an important message from Arlen. *(The Four Feathers)*

Powell, Clive Brook and Theodore Von Eltz, and is also tendered one by Wray, his wife, who is disillusioned with him.

Determined on self-redemption, Arlen goes to Africa; in an attempt to rescue Powell from a native fortress in the Sudan, he is himself captured and the two sold into the slave trade, but Arlen kills the slave trader and the natives pursue them. They weather other vicissitudes, including a hippo stampede, a bush fire and tribal hostility. Later Arlen has the chance to return all the feathers, the last one to Wray, He and his comrades are later decorated.

Lothar Mendes directed the interior scenes in Hollywood, but there was much location filming in Africa, courtesy of the documentary-turned-fiction team of Ernest B. Schoedsack and Merian C. Cooper. Some critics felt that possibly the full sound treatment, including dialogue. would have helped its box office

Powell and Brook discuss their cowardly ex-comrade. *(The Four Feathers)*

Powell ponders Arlen's defection in despair. *(The Four Feathers)*

99

in a sound-mad year. Powell was in and out in a supporting role, and had little to do as Captain Trench other than to glower, ponder and, occasionally, fight enemies. More than one critic considered his presence a waste.

CHARMING SINNERS

1929 PARAMOUNT

CAST:

Ruth Chatterton *(Kathryn Miles)*; Clive Brook *(Robert Miles)*; Mary Nolan *(Anne-Marie Whitley)*; William Powell *(Karl Kraley)*; Laura Hope Crews *(Mrs. Carr)*; Florence Eldridge *(Helen Carr)*; Montagu

Love *(George Whitley)*; Juliette Crosby *(Margaret)*; Lorraine Eddy *(Alice)*; Claude Allister *(Gregson)*.

CREDITS:

Robert Milton (Director); Doris Anderson (Screenplay/Adaptation); based on the play, *The Constant Wife* by W. Somerset Maugham; Victor Milner (Photographer); Verna Wills (Editor); Earl Hayman (Sound Engineer).

Running time, 8 reels. Released August 1929.

ESSAY

"Well-acted and intelligent," was *Photoplay's* verdict on *Charming Sinners*, a literate screen version (all-talkie) of *The Constant Wife*, the play in which Ethel Barrymore had made such a resounding hit in 1926. Some people wondered why Ethel herself had not been

Powell and Brook shake hands while Chatterton looks amused. *(Charming Sinners)*

Brook casts a jaundiced eye on Powell's handling of Chatterton. (*Charming Sinners*)

Advertising poster for *Charming Sinners.*

drafted for the talkie version, along with the original title, but the speaking screen would have to wait until 1932 to hear the famous Barrymore tones. Ruth Chatterton played the role on screen.

Powell was right in his element in this piece, in which his speaking voice was recorded to perfection, as a former admirer of a wife, Chatterton, who tolerates with mature objectivity the amorous dalliance of her husband, Clive Brook, with Mary Nolan. Chatterton encourages Powell's renewed suit, knowing it will annoy her erring husband and rekindle his interest, and when Brook and Nolan finally admit their adulterous involvement to Chatterton, her husband is so impressed by her dispassionate, logical reaction, that in his admiration for her he drops Nolan and returns to the marriage bed.

Ethel Barrymore and Company had given all this a civilized, ironic cast in the play, which had been one of W. Somerset Maugham's more polished confections, Ruth Chatterton, who had herself enjoyed no mean career in the theatre, and who was on the ascendant as one of the talkies' brightest new personalities, gave the role of the wisely detached and forgiving wife her own interpretation, and turned it into a major talkie hit in a performance on which the eminent Miss Barrymore could not have improved. Two other masters of the spoken word were, of course, Powell and Clive Brook, who did some classy verbal jousting as Chatterton's admirer and husband respectively.

The only drag on the proceedings was Mary Nolan, as the husband's inamorata, for she was not trained as thoroughly in stage deportment and speech as the others were, and the contrast showed at times rather glaringly. (Many wondered why a stage-trained actress had not been assigned to the role.) *Charming Sinners* got a charming reception from critics and public, and displayed Chatterton-Powell-Brook superbly in their element. Robert Milton, a director from the theatre, guided the principals.

THE GREENE MURDER CASE

1929 PARAMOUNT

CAST:

William Powell *(Philo Vance);* Florence Eldridge *(Sibella Greene);* Ullrich Haupt *(Dr. Von Blon);* Jean Arthur *(Ada Greene);* Eugene Pallette *(Sergeant Heath);* E. H. Calvert *(John F. X. Markham);* Gertrude Norman *(Mrs. Tobias Greene);* Lowell Drew *(Chester Greene);* Morgan Farley *(Rex Greene);* Brandon Hurst *(Sproot);* Augusta Burmeister *(Mrs. Mannheim);* Marcia Harris *(Hemming);* Mildred Golden *(Barton);* Mrs. Wilfred Buckland *(Nurse);* Helena Phillips *(Police Nurse);* Shep Camp *(Medical Examiner);* Charles E. Evans *(Lawyer Canon).*

CREDITS:

Frank Tuttle (Director); Louise Long (Screenplay); based on the story by S. S. Van Dine; Bartlett Cormack (Dialogue); Richard H. Digges, Jr. (Titles); Henry Gerrard (Photographer).

Running time, 8 reels. Released August 1929.

ESSAY

Powell had proven so popular as Philo Vance that within a few months he was again assigned to an S. S. Van Dine mystery, this time called *The Greene Murder Case.* Talented actress Florence Eldridge, who had come to Hollywood with her husband, Fredric March, to go into films, was on hand for this, as was Jean Arthur, who had been in the first Philo Vance film. This time around, director Frank Tuttle took the principals through their paces. Powell displayed in this, as in the first film, all his customary polish, authority and wisdom, nicely leavened with debonair humor.

E. H. Calvert as district attorney Markham (again) and police sergeant Eugene Pallette

"Put that gun down!" Powell commands. *(The Greene Murder Case)*

Florence Eldridge and Jean Arthur kibitz on Powell's sleuthing. *(The Greene Murder Case)*

(also again) enlist Vance's aid in solving the murder of one Chester Greene (Lowell Drew), who has been murdered, it would appear by a member of his own family. The hatred in the Greene family, of long-standing duration, comes immediately to the attention of Vance, who seeks to probe its ramifications. Two more members of the family go to their reward courtesy of the persistent murderer until the culprit (the last one the audience would suspect, naturally) dies in the East River while in the process of committing yet another homicide. All the usual clever red herrings and false alarms, at which Van Dine was the prime expert in his field, are paraded out, and Powell goes from clue to clue, alternating them with amusing exchanges with the dense Pallette, until the denouement. *Photoplay* called Powell "elegant," and the picture itself "fine."

There was much admiration in 1929-1930 for Powell's interpretation of Philo Vance, and S. S. Van Dine himself had reportedly expressed his wholehearted approval of Powell in the role. As to who committed the murder—just in case it should be revived—we won't spoil it for you by telling you. But it should come as one of the usual surprises of the kind only Van Dine could conceive, after spreading a delightful trail of confused alarms-and-excursions.

POINTED HEELS

1929 PARAMOUNT

CAST:

William Powell *(Robert Courtland);* Fay Wray *(Lora Nixon);* Helen Kane *(Dot Nixon);* Richard "Skeets" Gallagher *(Dash Nixon);* Phillips Holmes *(Donald Ogden);* Adrienne Dore *(Kay Wilcox);* Eugene Pallette *(Joe Clark).*

CREDITS:

A. Edward Sutherland (Director); Florence Ryerson, John V.A. Weaver (Adaptation/Dialogue); based on the story by Charles William Brackett; Perry Ivins (Dialogue Director); Rex Wimpy (Photographer); Jane Loring (Film Editor); Song: "I Have To Have You" by Richard A. Whiting and Leo Robin; Song: "Ain't-Cha?" by Mack Gordon and Max Rich. Movietone. Technicolor sequences.

Running time, 7 reels. Released December 1929.

ESSAY

Eddie Sutherland, always a director noted for his quick pacing and lively approach to the plot and casting, directed Powell in *Pointed Heels,* a story of the Broadway theatre with some Technicolor footage. The story was cinematized from a *College Humor* tale, and with him Powell had the lovely Fay Wray, who was fast on the rise as a leading lady, young Phillips Holmes, also becoming popular, and his old standby Eugene Pallette. Playing Wray's sister-in-law was singer Helen Kane, who sang some songs expertly without busting the re-

Wray and Holmes serve tea to Powell in their love nest. *(Pointed Heels)*

cording system, and who acted in a pert, jazzy style appropriate to her role. Richard "Skeets" Gallagher, always a dependable comedian, was Wray's brother.

A number of songs and lively musical numbers, some in the aforementioned Technicolor, were worked into the story. In it, Powell, as a classy, well-heeled theatrical producer, is working on a new musical comedy. Prominently spotted is Wray, in whom Powell has a romantic interest that is unreciprocated.

Wray decides that love is more important than career, and quits the show to marry composer Phillips Holmes. When his wealthy family cuts him off, Holmes and Wray are reduced to poverty, and she goes into a chorus line while he works on a symphony.

All ends well enough, with Holmes writing a popular song, Gallagher and Kane talking Powell into putting them in a new show; again trying to win Wray, Powell attempts to separate the pair, and almost succeeds until (of

Helen Kane spoofs with Powell while Gallagher watches ruefully. *(Pointed Heels)*

Wray relaxes in Powell's lavish penthouse. *(Pointed Heels)*

course) Holmes's song is the hit of the show and Wray goes back to him.

Director Sutherland kept the song numbers alternating neatly with the dialogue sequences, and the art director offers some interesting 1929-style contrasts between Powell's lavish penthouse and the humble little flat where Holmes and Wray play out their love.

Critics enthused over the Powell suavity and class, the Sutherland directorial pacing, and the nice songs. Helen Kane won special plaudits for her singing and amusing performance, though films were never to be a big factor in her career, unfortunately.

BEHIND THE MAKE-UP

1930 PARAMOUNT

CAST:

Hal Skelly *(Hap Brown);* William Powell *(Gardoni);* Fay Wray *(Marie);* Kay Francis *(Kitty Parker);* E. H. Calvert *(Dawson);* Paul Lukas *(Boris);* Agostino Borgato *(Chef);* Jacques Vanaire *(Valet);* Jean De Briac *(Sculptor).*

CREDITS:

Robert Milton (Director); George Manker Watters (Adaptation/Dialogue); Howard Estabrook (Co-Adaptor); Based on the story by Mildred Cram; Charles Lang (Photographer); Doris Drought (Editor); Songs: "My Pals," "Say It With Your Feet," "I'll Remember, You'll Forget" by Leo Robin, Sam Coslow, Newell Chase; Harry D. Mills (Sound).

Running time, 8 reels. Released January 1930.

ESSAY

"More backstage melodrama, but different and real this time," *Photoplay* said of Powell's first picture shown in 1930, *Behind the Makeup.* This was his first picture opposite Kay Francis, with whom he was to have a much-publicized romance, and he also had able co-stars in Hal Skelly and Fay Wray.

Skelly, Wray and Powell make a strange triangle. (*Behind the Makeup*)

Powell got billing above the title in this picture, directed by Robert Milton and based on a Mildred Cram story, *The Feeder,* which had appeared in a 1926 *Red Book.* The story has Skelly, an actor, falling deeply in love with Fay Wray, a waitress. Powell plays his egotistical partner, who cheats him out of the act in which they are appearing, forcing Skelly out. Later Powell steals Wray away from Skelly, causing the latter much heartbreak.

Powell later makes a success in New York, and cheats on wife Wray with racy man-eater Kay Francis. Powell is later deserted by Francis, thus getting his comeuppance, and he later dies. Skelly and Wray get back together again, and this time, under the inspiration of his newfound love, it is Skelly who wins major fame as a comedian.

The film purported to tell of all that goes on behind the scenes in the typical actor's life, with all the sudden friendships, equally sudden betrayals, quick romances—and, on occasion, enduring faithful love, which seems to be the exception rather than the rule, given the cynical nature of show business.

"Mr. Powell is most eloquent and restrained in this picture," one reviewer wrote, "appearing as both perpetrator and victim in the tournaments of the much-vaunted and much-overrated emotion known as love. His role has range and variety, and he plays off Miss Francis, Miss Wray and Mr. Skelly with the ease and authority of a seasoned trouper, carrying them along with him in a fine exhibition of first-class ensemble acting."

Powell seems to have felt that *Behind the Makeup*, despite its story limitations, took him several steps forward in the stellar leagues.

"Pagliacci"-type Skelly mourns over the Wray-Powell pairing. (*Behind the Makeup*)

Skelly seems to have gone to sleep on Powell and Wray. (*Behind the Makeup*)

Powell and Skelly are rivals in love and career. (*Behind the Makeup*)

Powell and Arthur want only the best for Toomey. *(Street of Chance)*

STREET OF CHANCE

1930 PARAMOUNT

CAST:

William Powell *(John B. Marsden/"Natural" Davis)*; Jean Arthur *(Judith Marsden)*; Kay Francis *(Alma Marsden)*; Regis Toomey *("Babe" Marsden)*; Stanley Fields *(Dorgan)*; Brooks Benedict *(Al Mastick)*; Betty Francisco *(Mrs. Mastick)*; John Risso *(Tony)*; Joan Standing *(Miss Abrams)*; Maurice Black *(Nick)*; Irving Bacon *(Harry)*; John Cromwell *(Imbrie)*.

CREDITS:

John Cromwell *(Director)*; Oliver H.P. Garrett *(Original Story)*; Lenore Coffee *(Dialogue)*; Gerald Geraghty *(Titles)*; Howard Estabrook *(Scenario/Adaptation)*; Charles Lang *(Photographer)*; Otto Levering *(Editor)*; Harry D. Mills *(Sound Engineer)*.

Running time, 9 reels. Released February 1930

ESSAY

Photoplay's reviewer wrote of Powell's second 1930 release, *Street of Chance*: "Here's a punchful racketeer picture that is going to give rival producers jaundice until they get a carbon copy in the can. Bill Powell's finesse and Kay Francis's sincere emoting would be highlights in any picture."

Kay Francis was Powell's leading lady in what was his best opportunity to that date to shift from villain to hero in the audience's mind (up to then, they had associated him more with the former than the latter). The story, carefully tailored to Powell's talents, won an Academy Award nomination for Howard Estabrook, who adapted it from a story by Oliver H.P. Garrett, based in part on the life story of famous and/or notorious gambler Arnold Rothstein, a colorful New York figure of the 1920's.

The *Photoplay* review had set the keynote for the flood of laudatory notices Powell received for a role that enhanced his prominence immeasurably and caused Paramount to seriously regard him as a major star-to-be. As written, it contained all the worldly wise knowledgeableness and savoir-faire that the fans had come to treasure in Powell's performances.

Here he is on display as John Marsden, a feared and respected New York gambler noted for copping big stakes and for his sharpshooting feats. He is devoted to his wife,

Kay Francis, and his younger brother, Regis Toomey. Francis wants him to quit gambling and settle down to a quiet life. This he promises to do, once he has won a large-enough stake. He gives his brother a wedding present of $10,000 for his marriage to Jean Arthur, but on the condition that Toomey will avoid a gambler's career, for which he is already displaying a burgeoning obsession.

To teach his brother a lesson, however, Powell cheats for the first time in a game in which Toomey is betting heavily and recklessly, and is caught by the gamblers, who kill him.

Street of Chance was the first released film to display the winning romantic duo of Powell and Francis, who were to do other interesting films together later.

Powell tries to soothe a worried Francis. *(Street of Chance)*

Looks like Natalie Moorhead is high on Powell's suspect list. *(The Benson Murder Case)*

THE BENSON MURDER CASE

1930 PARAMOUNT

CAST:

William Powell *(Philo Vance)*; Natalie Moorhead *(Fanny Del Roy)*; Eugene Pallette *(Sergeant Heath)*; Paul Lukas *(Adolph Mohler)*; William Boyd *(Harry Gray)*; E.H. Calvert *(John F.X. Markham)*; Richard Tucker *(Anthony Benson)*; May Beatty *(Mrs. Paula Banning)*; Mischa Auer *(Albert)*; Otto Yamaoka *(Sam;* Charles McMurphy *(Burke)*; Dick Rush *(Welch)*.

CREDITS:

Frank Tuttle *(Director)*; Bartlett Cormack *(Scenario/Dialogue)*; Perry Ivins *(Dialogue Director)*;

A.J. Stout (Photographer); Doris Drought (Editor); Harold M. McNiff (Sound Recording). Movietone.

Running time, 7 reels. Released April 1930.

ESSAY

For his third time around as Philo Vance, his ever-more-popular detective role, Powell sets out to solve the murder of a wealthy stockbroker who sold out several people during the 1929 market crash. Richard Tucker is the stockbroker; William Boyd a gambler who was one of his victims; as were Natalie Moorhead, a Broadway actress whose jewels were stolen to redeem a check; Paul Lukas, a forged-check holder; and May Beatty, a widow in love with Benson.

The action takes place at Tucker's hunting lodge some miles from New York, where visitors Powell and E.H. Calvert, playing District Attorney Markham, set out to unravel the conflicting, red-herring clues and find the correct line that leads to the murderer.

Looks like Moorhead has been into pearl-mischief here. *(The Benson Murder Case)*

Powell rounds up suspects Moorhead, Lukas *et al.* in E.H. Calvert's office. *(The Benson Murder Case)*

Pallette, Powell and Calvert seem to have hit on a clue. *(The Benson Murder Case)*

Powell is his usual suave self here, with Calvert and Eugene Pallette, as Sergeant Heath, his ably depicted allies and/or foils. There are the usual false alarms and likely suspects. The murderer in time turns out to be Boyd, who is shot as he attempts a getaway.

Photoplay reacted thus: "Another elegant Van Dine murder mystery. Suave Bill Powell . . . gets his man. See it." (When *Photoplay* tacked on the "see it" tag, it usually meant that the film had a sound approval rating from what was then America's most influential film publication.)

The action was quick and economical, as guided by director Frank Tuttle, and was based on S.S. Van Dine's 1926 novel of the same name. Some reviewers thought it *too* quick, and it was dubbed a "quickie" in some circles, designed to capitalize both on Powell's growing popularity (especially after *Street of Chance*) and on the Philo Vance vogue then raging.

Powell himself, in a 1930 interview, gave it as his view that the Philo Vance craze would not last forever; he said he hoped the studio wouldn't make too much of a good thing, and that perhaps they ought to quit while they were ahead. The studio then proceeded to produce a Spanish-language version, thus assuring even more profits for their 1930 balance sheets.

PARAMOUNT ON PARADE

1930 PARAMOUNT

CAST:

Included Iris Adrian, Richard Arlen, Jean Arthur, Mischa Auer, William Austin, George Bancroft, Clara Bow, Evelyn Brent, Mary Brian, Clive Brook, Virginia Bruce, Nancy Carroll, Ruth Chatterton, Maurice Chevalier, Gary Cooper, Cecil Cunningham, Leon Errol, Stuart Erwin, Henry Fink, Kay Francis, Skeets Gallagher, Edmund Goulding, Harry Green, Mitzi Green, Robert Greig, James Hall, Phillips Holmes, Helen Kane, Dennis King, Abe Lyman and his Band, Fredric March, Nino Martini, Mitzi Mayfair, Marion Morgan Dancers, David Newell, Jack Oakie, Warner Oland, Zelma O'Neal, Eugene Pallette, Joan Peers, Jack Pennick, William Powell, Charles (Buddy) Rogers, Lillian Roth, Rolfe Sedan, Stanley Smith, Fay Wray.

CREDITS:

Dorothy Arzner, Otto Brower, Edmund Goulding, Victor Heerman, Edwin H. Knopf, Rowland V. Lee, Ernst Lubitsch, Lothar Mendes, Victor Schertzinger, Edward Sutherland, Frank Tuttle (Directors); Harry Fischbeck, Victor Milner (Photographers); John Wenger (Set Designs.) Numerous song numbers courtesy of Elsie Janis, Jack King, Ballard MacDonald, Dave Dreyer, Leo Robin, Ernesto De Curtis, L. Wolfe Gilbert, Abel Baer, Richard A. Whiting, Raymond B. Eagan, Sam Coslow; David Bennett (Dance Director). Some Technicolor Sequences. Movietone.

Running time, 13 reels. Released May, 1930.

ESSAY

Paramount on Parade was one of those all-star efforts so popular at the time, and featuring—in a 13-reel running time—a number of musical numbers, skits and assorted spoofings. Elsie Janis, the famed World War I entertainer, was listed as the "supervisor," with the basic direction entrusted to pioneer female director Dorothy Arzner, along with such worthies as Edmund Goulding, Edwin H. Knopf, Rowland V. Lee, Ernst Lubitsch, Edward Sutherland and Frank Tuttle. Among the song numbers were a "Paramount on Parade Theme Song," "What Did Cleopatra Say?", "Let Us Drink to the Girl of My Dreams," "My Marine," and the famed "Sweepin' The Clouds Away," courtesy of such song-and-lyric heavyweights as Leo Robin, Richard A. Whiting, Sam Coslow and Jack King. Among the top Paramount stars represented in various songs and skits were Clara Bow, Evelyn Brent, Kay Francis, Charles (Buddy) Rogers, Nancy Carroll, Ruth Chatterton, Fredric March—and Powell, (as Philo Vance), Clive Brook (as Sherlock Holmes) and

Note "Philo Vance" Powell and "Sherlock Holmes" Brook behind the "E" in the *Paramount on Parade* line-up. (*Paramount on Parade*)

Warner Oland (as Fu Manchu) involved in an amusing skit that was one of the highlights of the all-star presentation.

An excerpt from *Photoplay*'s verdict: "Paramount goes revue, using its best talent, Technicolor, stirring music, lovely voices, satire, burlesque, romance!"

Metro-Goldwyn-Mayer and Warner Bros. had already pre-empted this particular genre respectively with *The Hollywood Revue* and *The Show of Shows,* and some reviewers felt that *Paramount on Parade* was too much of a good thing in more ways than one.

Powell, however, displayed a sharp sense of humor and meticulous comic timing in his thorough spoofing of his Philo Vance character; given the crowded goings-on, his running time was not long, but he made the most of it. By 1930 the all-star item was for the time played out, and none of the big studios chose to repeat it in a similar format.

The Powell-Brook-Oland skit was called *Murder Will Out,* and included Jack Oakie as the "victim," with Eugene Pallette adding to the hilarity with a takeoff on his amusing "Sergeant Heath" character.

115

SHADOW OF THE LAW

1930 PARAMOUNT

CAST:

William Powell *(John Nelson/Jim Montgomery);* Marion Shilling *(Edith Wentworth);* Natalie Moorhead *(Ethel Barry);* Regis Toomey *(Tom);* Paul Hurst *(Pete);* George Irving *(Colonel Wentworth);* Frederic Burt *(Mike Kearney);* James Durkin *(Warden);* Richard Tucker *(Frank);* Walter James *(Guard Captain).*

CREDITS:

Louis Gasnier *(Director);* John Farrow *(Scenario/Dialogue);* based on *The Quarry* by John A. Moroso; Charles Lang *(Photographer);* Robert Bassler *(Editor);* Harold M. McNiff *(Sound).*

Running time, 7 reels. Released June 1930.

ESSAY

Shadow of the Law was a remake of a 1921 film, *The City of Silent Men.* (It is not to be confused with a 1926 silent starring Clara Bow, which was called *The Shadow of the Law.*) Powell's 1930 film was based on an original by John Moroso, called *The Quarry* (1913).

Photoplay wrote of this: "The usual delightful William Powell performance, but the story could be better." The story that the magazine's reviewer thought not up to snuff dealt with Powell, an engineer whose apartment is invaded by a lady (Natalie Moorhead) who is in flight from a drunken man who, upon being challenged by Powell, accidentally falls to his death from the engineer's window.

The woman disappears and, because he has no witness, Powell is convicted on circumstantial evidence and sentenced to life imprisonment. Later, he manages to escape, disguises his identity, and goes to the South, where he eventually becomes the manager of a textile mill. He tries to find Moorhead so that he can

Moorhead is up to no good here with Powell. *(Shadow of the Law)*

Powell and Marion Shilling find their love threatened. (*Shadow of the Law*)

be cleared in order to marry Marion Shilling, the mill owner's daughter, but instead the unscrupulous Moorhead tries to blackmail him. Events favor him, and he is eventually cleared.

Most reviewers seemed to agree with *Photoplay* that *Shadow of the Law*, directed by Louis Gasnier from a John Farrow scenario, was not the strongest vehicle for Powell, what with its forced situations and telescoped events, to say nothing of considerably stretched coincidences, but all agreed that the star made the proceedings look more weighty than they actually were.

"Even in somewhat superficial melodrama like this, Mr. Powell forces us not only to like him, but to root for him; such is the power of a good actor who knows his business to elicit affirmative reactions even in the face of unworthy material," one reviewer stated. Which about sums up what most critics across the country in 1930 thought of *Shadow of the Law* and William Powell.

It looks like trouble is brewing for Powell, Moorhead and Tucker. (*Shadow of the Law*)

Regis Toomey, Natalie Moorhead and Powell relax on the set. *(Shadow of the Law)*

FOR THE DEFENSE

1930 PARAMOUNT

CAST:

William Powell *(William Foster);* Kay Francis *(Irene Manners);* Scott Kolk *(Defoe);* William B. Davidson *(District Attorney Stone);* John Elliott *(McGann);* Thomas Jackson *(Daly);* Harry Walker *(Miller);* James Finlayson *(Parrott);* Charles West *(Joe);* Charles Sullivan *(Charlie);* Ernest Adams *(Eddie Withers);* Bertram Marburgh *(Judge Evans);* Edward Le Saint *(Judge).*

CREDITS:

John Cromwell (Director); Oliver H.P. Garrett (Scenario/Dialogue); Charles Furthman (Original Story); Charles Lang (Photographer); George Nichols, Jr. (Editor); Harold M. McNiff (Sound).

Running time, 7 reels. Released July 1930.

ESSAY

In *For the Defense,* Powell is a famous and successful criminal lawyer who specializes in getting assorted clients off the hook. Thomas Jackson, a canny detective, is investigating him. Powell is involved with actress Kay Francis, but feels he is not the marrying kind, hence avoids the altar. This miffs Francis, who takes up with a worthless playboy. Driving the

Francis seems worried by Powell's disapproval. *(For the Defense)*

William B. Davidson and Francis ponder Powell's dilemma. *(For the Defense)*

Powell and Francis are lost in a world of their own. *(For the Defense)*

playboy's car on the way home from a roadhouse, Francis kills a pedestrian. The playboy takes the blame, and Powell is assigned to defend him. When Powell learns that Francis, in fact, is the one guilty of manslaughter, he bribes a juror to plump for a hung jury.

Jackson tracks down the evidence of Powell's bribery attempt and the latter is arrested. Francis goes to the district attorney and almost confesses her guilt. But Powell admits his guilt in the bribery action, and when he goes to prison, Francis promises to wait for him.

The convolutions and fuzzy morality implicit in this story by Charles Furthman with a scenario by Oliver H. P. Garrett is cleverly disguised by the able direction of John Cromwell, and the film turned out to be one of Powell's biggest hits. *Photoplay* tended to dismiss it with the single word *Good*, but other reviewers hailed it as a fine starring vehicle for Powell.

Shot by Cromwell in only three weeks, and based reportedly on the career of attorney William Fallon, a New York attorney who later

Has Powell got Francis behind the proverbial eight-ball? *(For the Defense)*

was the model for a Warners film called *The Mouthpiece, For the Defense* did surprisingly well at the boxoffice, and helped put the William Powell-Kay Francis team into a pairing category that by 1932 would almost (at the time) equal in popularity the later teaming of William Powell and Myrna Loy.

Sophisticated, suspenseful and well-paced, *For the Defense* assured Powell's position as Paramount's top boxoffice star for 1930.

MAN OF THE WORLD

1931 PARAMOUNT

CAST:

William Powell *(Michael Wagstag)*; Carole Lombard *(Mary Kendall)*; Wynne Gibson *(Irene)*; Guy Kibbee *(Harold Taylor)*; Lawrence Gray *(Frank Thompson)*; Tom Ricketts *(Mr. Bradkin)*; Andre Cheron *(Victor)*; George Chandler *(Fred)*; Tom Costello *(Spade)*; Maud Truax *(Mrs. Jowitt)*.

CREDITS:

Richard Wallace and Edward Goodman (Directors); Herman J. Mankiewicz (Story and Screenplay); Victor Milner (Photographer); H.M. Lindgren (Sound).

Running time, 74 minutes. Released March 1931.

ESSAY

Man of the World was the first of Powell's three pictures with Carole Lombard, whom he married in 1931, the year of the picture's release. They met while making this film, and he is said to have mentored acting tricks that helped her sparkle in this.

The film was standard romantic silliness, given unwarranted substance by Powell's sincere and realistic performance. In this he is a mountebank who specializes in blackmailing wealthy American innocents who come to Paris seeking glamour and romance. He tries

his wiles on debutante Lombard, but soon finds himself falling in love with her. His interest is returned.

But there is a hitch; he has employed as his confederate in his nefarious schemes a hard cookie, Wynne Gibson, who tells him that he can never reform his life at that late date and attempts to keep him in line by a threat to inform on him to the police.

Soon, egged on by Gibson, Powell reverts partially to his cynical attitude toward life and people, despairing of ever finding a future with Lombard. Soon he is trying to extract thousands of dollars from Guy Kibbee, Lombard's uncle, and when she learns of this the disillusioned young lady decides to sail back to America.

Powell and Gibson, recognizing that they are two of a kind, board a tramp steamer heading for South America, but en route,

Powell is in more than a soup-eating contest with Lawrence Gray, while Lombard tries to catch up. *(Man of the World)*

Wynne Gibson is determined that Powell should accept reality. *(Man of the World)*

Powell and Wynne Gibson live in a fool's paradise—for the moment. *(Man of the World)*

Powell, realizing that he has lost his last chance for genuine love, destroys Kibbee's check for the money he has swindled.

"Competently acted," *The New York Times* declared, "particularly by Mr. Powell." Carole Lombard got off with "Beautiful." And from the influential James R. Quirk of *Photoplay:* "A good picture; not much action but plenty of drama and a great performance by William Powell."

The Powell-Lombard romance accelerated during the making of this film. Soon they were to do another.

Powell is smitten with Lombard's charms. *(Ladies' Man)*

Powell is equally adored by Francis and Lombard. *(Ladies' Man)*

LADIES' MAN

1931 PARAMOUNT

CAST:

William Powell *(James Darricott)*; Kay Francis *(Norma Page)*; Carole Lombard *(Rachel Fendley)*; Gilbert Emery *(Horace Fendley)*; Olive Tell *(Mrs. Fendley)*; Martin Burton *(Anthony Fendley)*; John Holland *(Peyton Weldon)*; Frank Atkinson *(Valet)*; Manda Turner Gordon *(Therese Bianton)*.

CREDITS:

Lothar Mendes (Director); Herman J. Mankiewicz (Screenplay and Dialogue); based on a story by Rupert Hughes; Victor Milner (Photographer); H.M. Lindgreen (Recording Engineer).

Running time, 70 minutes. Released May 1931.

ESSAY

Powell had in *Ladies' Man* two women with whom he had had an intimate offscreen association, and one of whom he married: Kay Francis and Carole Lombard. Powell and Lombard were married six weeks after this film's official release.

Again, Powell is a rascal with the Ladies, this time specializing in entertaining wealthy bored wives and living off the proceeds of the expensive presents they give him. Olive Tell, a lady of uncertain age who is determined on a romantic fling despite her advancing years, is one of his admirers. Her daughter, Lombard, who knows what is going on, at first despises, then falls in love with, Powell.

But even scoundrels know the pangs and transports of true love, and for Powell this resides in the person of Kay Francis. Mean-

Francis knows she's Powell's true love. *(Ladies' Man)*

while socialite millionaire Gilbert Emery, learning of his wife Tell's involvement with Powell, confronts him in his apartment, and Powell accidentally falls to his death from the window, with Emery surrendering to the police. Thus neither of the ladies wins Powell for their own, which in both cases is just as well, considering the character of James Darricott as expertly limned by Powell and as written by Herman Mankiewicz. All this was directed by Lothar Mendes, who by this time had become an expert with such stories.

Photoplay called Powell "a sympathetic and attractive gigolo," and other reviewers praised his "poise," "suavity" and "tactful but pointed thespic maneuverings in a role not too likeable but made interesting due to the Powell charm."

At this time, Powell expressed to interviewers some worry that he would become "typed" as the 1931 version of the snaky heel who is poison to women who care for him, but his inherent versatility was to overcome that in short order.

Carole Lombard, responding to his tutoring, delivered a delightful performance in this film, with reviewers commenting on her growing poise and chic.

Powell plays with Lombard's affections. *(Ladies' Man)*

THE ROAD TO SINGAPORE

1931 WARNER BROS.

CAST:

William Powell *(Hugh Dawltry);* Doris Kenyon *(Philippa Crosby);* Marian Marsh *(Rene);* Alison Skipworth *(Mrs. Wey-Smith);* Louis Calhern *(Dr. George March);* Lumsden Hare *(Mr. Wey Smith);* Ethel Griffies *(Mrs. Everard);* A.E. Anson *(Dr. Muir).*

CREDITS:

Alfred E. Green (Director); J. Grubb Alexander (Screenplay); based on a play by Roland Pertwee and a story by Denis Robins.

Running time, 75 minutes. Released October 1931.

Powell is talking Doris Kenyon into something, obviously. *(Road to Singapore)*

Husband Louis Calhern glowers at wife Kenyon as she dances with Powell. *(Road to Singapore)*

Powell and Marian Marsh indulge in some horseplay. (*Road to Singapore*)

Powell is up to no good with Kenyon, another man's wife. (*Road to Singapore*)

ESSAY

The Road to Singapore was Powell's first picture under his new Warners contract, but it turned out to be rather perfunctory and falsely melodramatic stuff under the less-than-inspired direction of Alfred E. Green; it was based on a play by Roland Pertwee.

As if Warners knew it had a platitudinous collection of melodramatic clichés on its hands, it even threw in some badly executed songs, including such dillies as "Just a Fool in Love With You," "Yes or No," "Singapore Tango" and "Hand in Hand."

This time around, Powell is a cad (of sorts) out to seduce the wife of a doctor, Louis Calhern. The hapless wife, Doris Kenyon, finds herself even kidnapped (if that is the term) to Powell's house on a tropical island. Of course she doesn't love her boorish, insensitive spouse, who has love at the bottom of his priorities, and she returns to Powell after initially escaping. It seems that love has re-

129

deemed Powell, and he promises to be a cad no more.

The critics were not impressed by this artificial concoction, which they deemed short on fresh dramatic values and long on clichés. "We had expected more from Mr. Powell's shift to Warners, and we don't understand why the studio couldn't have come up with something more suitable to welcome his advent," one critic said.

And from another: "Mr. Powell does as well as he can with what the screenplay and Alfred E. Green's direction have provided, but even his sharp energies, high spirits and ability to make something out of nothing are sorely put to the test here."

Louis Calhern, though cast as the outraged cuckold who discovers his wife's dalliance with Powell, gave a sinister twist to the doings though cast as the gentleman technically in the right; and Doris Kenyon, a lovely blond star who had won top fame in the silents, acquitted herself well as the lady caught between opposing poles, so to speak. But none of it did anything to advance Powell's career.

HIGH PRESSURE

1932 WARNER BROS.

CAST:

William Powell *(Gar Evans)*; Evelyn Brent *(Francine)*; George Sidney *(Ginsberg)*; Guy Kibbee *(Clifford)*; Evalyn Knapp *(Helen)*; John Wray *(Jimmy Moore)*; Frank McHugh *(Mike)*; Polly Walters *(Millie)*; Ben Alexander *(Geoffrey)*.

CREDITS:

Mervyn LeRoy *(Director)*; Joseph Jackson *(Screenplay)*; based on a play by Aben Kandel; Robert Kurrle *(Photographer)*.

Running time, 72 minutes. Released March 1932.

ESSAY

For his second Warner picture, Powell drew Mervyn LeRoy as director and a fast-paced and at times inventive screenplay by Joseph Jackson, based on a play by Aben Kandel.

Sensing that Powell's first picture for Warners, *The Road to Singapore*, had been an unworthy showcase for his stellar talents, for which they were paying him a fabulous weekly salary courtesy of his high-powered agent, the producers went all-out to make *High Pressure* a picture worthy of its title in every way.

Ben Alexander seems to be stirring up some dust for Powell, Evalyn Knapp and Evelyn Brent. *(High Pressure)*

That they succeeded, at least in part, was attested by the better-than-average reviews cross-country, which featured such reactions as "highly entertaining," "amusingly fast-paced," "deftly acted" and "likeable."

The story has Powell as an ambitious, and inventive, promoter trying to break into high finance and big business by any means possible. He decides that artificial rubber is the ticket, and forms a rather rickety but well-hyped firm called The Golden Gate Artificial Rubber Company.

Powell thinks his high-pressure tactics have really put him into high gear this time around,

Evalyn Knapp follows Powell's dictation closely. (*High Pressure*)

after a past of near misses and assorted false alarms, but it turns out that Harry Beresford, who invented the product on which everything stands or falls, has done a disappearing act. How Powell maneuvers his way around this disaster makes for some entertaining results. In a role that seems to be tailored to the measure of Lee Tracy, Powell puts over his own approach, loading the part with personality and inventive nuance. LeRoy, as director, provides a fast pace and a sparkling style, for felicitous results.

Evelyn Brent, looking rather tired and her lustre of the Paramount days somewhat depleted, is on hand as Powell's love interest (reportedly at his request, so as to revive her flagging fortunes circa 1932), and Frank McHugh, Guy Kibbee and Evalyn Knapp lend sterling support.

Powell reportedly felt it represented an improvement over his first Warners effort.

Evelyn Brent and Powell in a light moment. *(High Pressure)*

Frank McHugh wonders what Brent and Powell are up to. *(High Pressure)*

Powell and Francis pitch some woo. (*Jewel Robbery*)

JEWEL ROBBERY

1932 WARNER BROS.

Running time, 68 minutes. Released July 1932

CAST:

William Powell *(The Robber);* Kay Francis *(Baroness Teri von Horhenfels);* Hardie Albright *(Paul);* Andre Luguet *(Count Andre);* Henry Kolker *(Baron Franz von Horhenfels);* Spencer Charters *(Johann Christian Lenz);* Alan Mowbray *(Fritz);* Helen Vinson *(Marianne);* Lawrence Grant *(Professor Bauman);* Jacques Vanaire *(Manager);* Harold Minjur *(Clark);* Ivan Linow *(Chauffeur);* Charles Coleman *(Charles);* Ruth Donnelly *(Berta);* Clarence Wilson *(The Commissioner);* Leo White *(Assistant Robber);* Donald Brodie, Eddie Kane *(Robbers);* Gordon Elliott *(Gendarme).*

CREDITS:

William Dieterle (Director); Erwin Gelsey (Screenplay); based on the play by Ladislaus Fodor; Robert Kurrle (Photographer); Ralph Dawson (Editor).

ESSAY

Jewel Robbery displayed Powell, on yet another outing with Kay Francis, as a suave jewel thief in Vienna who regards his takings as works of art, and who brings an artist's appreciation to his clever schemes. Francis is the bored and unhappy Baroness married to stuffy Henry Kolker, and of course she and Powell, robberies and assorted chicaneries notwithstanding, are fated to meet and love.

The proceedings called out—*cried* out, for that matter—for the Lubitsch touch, and instead had to settle for the services of William Dieterle, at his best in costume epics and at his weakest in frothy confections like this. James Robert Parish has pointed out that 1932 audiences were particularly thrilled by a scene in which a cigarette filled with marijuana was passed about, as marijuana was an exciting novelty at that time, though familiar enough later.

Powell's in trouble with Alan Mowbray and the police, but Francis loves him anyway. (*Jewel Robbery*)

The screenplay by Erwin Gelsey was amusing enough, and in Lubitsch's hands might have been altogether captivating. Based on a play by Ladislaus Fodor, *Jewel Robbery* contained equal doses of light romancing and clever skullduggery, and Powell sparkled, as always, as a man irresistible to women who dares to aspire to a Baroness's affections. Though Francis was not at her best in this (she needed special handling—meaning Lubitsch's—to register in subtle froth like this), she did follow Powell's lead sufficiently to emerge as competent in most critics' estimation.

The Gelsey-cum-Fodor lines were amusing,

and well-tailored to the characters, but the plot was predictable enough, having been given a run-through by many a writer in the past, but the atmosphere of Vienna was well-conveyed, even though no one got a step off the Warner sound stages and back lots in Burbank.

One critic wrote: "Mr. Powell must get mightily tired of pouring on the charm, but on the surface he gives no indication of it here, and Kay Francis, while not quite up to his standards, gives a competent rendition of a noblewoman smitten to the point of indiscretion."

134

Powell and Francis see something they like, obviously. (*Jewel Robbery*)

Hardie Albright at the point of a gun, as Powell watches. (*Jewel Robbery*)

ONE WAY PASSAGE

1932   WARNER BROS.

CAST:

William Powell *(Dan Hardesty)*; Kay Francis *(Joan Ames)*; Frank McHugh *(Skippy)*; Aline MacMahon *(Betty)*; Warren Hymer *(Steve Burke)*; Frederick Burton *(Doctor)*; Douglas Gerrard *(Sir Harold)*; Herbert Mundin *(Steward)*; Wilson Mizner *(Singing Drunk)*; Mike Donlin *(Hong Kong Bartender)*; Roscoe Karns *(Ship's Bartender)*; Dewey Robinson *(Honolulu Contact)*; Bill Halligan *(Agua Caliente Bartender)*; Willie Fung *(Curio Dealer)*; Stanley Fields *(Captain)*; Heinie Conklin *(Singer)*; Allan Lane, Ruth Hall *(Friends)*; Harry Seymour *(Ship's Officer)*.

CREDITS:

Tay Garnett (Director); Robert Lord (Story); Wilson Mizner, Joseph Jackson (Screenplay); Robert Kurrle (Photographer); Ralph Dawson (Editor).

Running time, 69 minutes. Released September, 1932.

ESSAY

One-Way Passage, the sixth and last film Powell made with Kay Francis, was their greatest success—in fact, the greatest success either was to know at Warners. A hokey but poignant tale about a convict on his way to the electric chair and a playgirl who has learned she is dying of heart disease, who meet and romance on a boat ploughing from Hong Kong to San Francisco, it made quite an impression on 1932 audiences, who closed their eyes deliberately to the hokey contrivances and allowed themselves to be swept along in the romantic flood. Especially popular was the closing shot, in a bar in Agua Caliente, where two champagne glasses are mysteriously broken on New Year's eve, with the stems crossed, to the perplexity of the bartenders.

The "plant" for this was that earlier in the film, Powell and Francis had made a New Year's Eve date for that Agua Caliente bar, but by the time it came around, they were both dead. Their "ghosts" did the trick for them, anyway, and audiences exited weeping over this contrived but effective final poignancy.

On hand were such expert comedian supports as Aline MacMahon and Frank McHugh, and Tay Garnett did a highly professional job of extracting all the tears that the story warranted. Wilson Mizner and Joseph Jackson, the screenwriters, made the most of the basic original story provided by Robert Lord, with every second of the 69 minutes of running time a pay-off.

Director Tay Garnett has told amusing stories of the revamping of the dialogue to disguise Kay Francis's celebrated speech impediment (her r's came out like w's, and she made it, in time, her trademark) He was particularly amused by her recitation of one line: "It wouldn't be wight, even if we ah in wuv." (Her l's weren't so hot, either.)

Photoplay enthused: "By far the best movie that Kay Francis and William Powell have turned out as a team." Other critics were equally enthusiastic, and the public turned out in droves. *One-Way Passage* was remade,

Warren Hymer keeps Powell on the cuffs. *(One Way Passage)*

Powell and Kay Francis enjoy the breezes. *(One Way Passage)*

An intimate moment between Powell and Francis. *(One Way Passage)*

Warren Hymer breaks up an impending clinch between Powell and Francis. *(One Way Passage)*

unsuccessfully, as *Till We Meet Again* (1940), with Merle Oberon and George Brent.

LAWYER MAN

1932   WARNER BROS.

CAST:

William Powell *(Anton Adam);* Joan Blondell *(Olga);* Helen Vinson *(Barbara Bentley);* Allan Dinehart *(Granville Bentley);* Allen Jenkins *(Issy Levine);* David Landau *(Gilmurry);* Claire Dodd *(Virginia);* Sheila Terry *(Flo);* Jack LaRue (Spike).

CREDITS:

William Dieterle (Director); James Seymour (Screenplay); Rian James (Associate on Screenplay); based on the novel by Max Trell.

Running time, 72 minutes. Released December 1932.

David Landau doesn't seem to have time for Sheila Terry, and what will Powell do with Claire Dodd? *(Lawyer Man)*

ESSAY

Lawyer Man was a pleasant-enough entertainment from the Warner sound stages, and while it didn't stretch Powell's acting talents much, it provided him with some escapist stuff in which he proves that an ambitious New York lawyer might be something of a cad but amusing and likeable nonetheless—a character (and a genre) in which he was more than a little experienced by then.

Joan Blondell, as his scretary, was mightily amusing in her usual fey style, and her chemistry blended well with Powell's, though some Powell fans felt they made a strange combination. "Powell acts primarily with his intellect, Blondell with her instincts," one reviewer wrote, "but the surprise is that they blend so well considering they are coming from opposite corners with what you would *think* would be conflicting acting styles."

William Dieterle was on hand again, and since the humor was more direct and heavy-handed this time around, with no necessity for

139

Powell and Joan Blondell at comic odds. (*Lawyer Man*)

gossamer subtleties, he kept it moving with reasonable facility.

Based on a novel by Max Trell, with a screenplay from the typewriters of Rian James and Max Trell, *Lawyer Man* had to do with an ambitious lawyer who rises from mouthpiece for the Lower East Side underprivileged to the almost-heights as an assistant prosecutor. He runs afoul of Claire Dodd (who ran neck-and-neck with Gail Patrick as Man-Trouble to many a male star of the 1930's) and finds himself nailed for blackmail. A hung jury gets him off, and he escapes prosecution.

These are the bare bones of the story, but Powell makes the circuitous doings seem much more exciting and engrossing than they actually are. Dieterle's direction, and such able ensemble players as Alan Dinehart, David Landau, Allen Jenkins, and another Dodd-Patrick rival for the title of Miss Man-Trouble,

Powell and Blondell look puzzled by the old gentleman. (*Lawyer Man*)

Blondell doesn't seem amused by Powell's clowning. *(Lawyer Man)*

Helen Vinson has Powell's attention while Blondell sulks. *(Lawyer Man)*

Helen Vinson, keeping things percolating professionally.

"There is nothing heavyweight about this," one reviewer opined, "but who cares as long as Bill Powell is on hand to keep the top spinning—and spin it does!"

PRIVATE DETECTIVE 62

1933 WARNER BROS.

CAST:

William Powell *(Donald)*; Margaret Lindsay *(Janet)*; Ruth Donnelly *(Amy)*; Gordon Westcott *(Bandor)*; James Bell *(Whitey)*; Arthur Byron *(Tracey)*; Natalie Moorhead *(Mrs. Burns)*; Sheila Terry *(The Girl)*; Theresa Harris *(Maid)*; Revel Whitney *(Alice)*; Hobart Cavanaugh *(Burns)*; Arthur Hohl *(Rogan)*.

CREDITS:

Michael Curtiz *(Director)*; Hal Wallis *(Supervisor)*; Rian James *(Screenplay)*; based on a story by Raoul Whitfield. Original title: *Man Killer*.

Running time, 67 minutes. Released July 1933.

ESSAY

Private Detective 62, in which Powell had the benefit of Michael Curtiz's fast-paced, no-nonsense direction, was no world-beater, but a snappy, fast-paced screenplay by Rian James, perfectly tailored to Curtiz's directorial style (James's effort was based on a story by Raoul Whitfield), brought good boxoffice and fairly good critical results.

Some 1933 critics, however, felt that Powell's talent was not being mounted as well at Warners as it had been at Paramount. "Mr. Powell has become an expert at making trivia look reasonably intelligent, even significant, and while his special talents are taxed perhaps more than usual by *Private Detective 62*, he

Toasting lovely Margaret Lindsay. *(Private Detective 62)*

Powell bewilders Ruth Donnelly and Arthur Hohl with cash. *(Private Detective 62)*

does bring off the slight proceedings more successfully than one would think," one reviewer stated.

The melodramatic proceedings have Powell, a former agent of the U.S. foreign service, becoming a private detective—number 62, naturally—and falling in love with Margaret Lindsay, a lovely lady with an unfortunate fondness for the gambling tables. Soon Powell is forced by his client to investigate Lindsay's activities, with Arthur Hohl, one of the most popular heavies of the 1930's, on hand to provide negative obstacles to the progress of the Powell-Lindsay love affair.

Needless to say, Powell eventually gets everything straightened out, both in his love

affair with Lindsay and his conflicts with Hohl.

Ruth Donnelly, Gordon Westcott, Arthur Byron and Natalie Moorhead (Powell's old colleague from Paramount) offer able supporting performances, and Curtiz doesn't waste a minute. Margaret Lindsay was a beautiful Warners leading lady who, however, was unsure of her acting talents. Always modest, self-effacing and unassuming (rare qualities

Natalie Moorhead and Lindsay seem to have Powell off-balance. (*Private Detective 62*)

Powell gets Arthur Hohl in line as Lindsay and James Bell look on. (*Private Detective 62*)

143

indeed in a member of the acting profession), Lindsay later told an interviewer that Powell in *Private Detective 62* and Bette Davis in the 1938 *Jezebel* were two performers from whom she learned just by playing off their expertise. This film is never revived and is almost unknown to all but Powell enthusiasts.

DOUBLE HARNESS

1933   RKO-RADIO

CAST:

Ann Harding *(Joan Colby)*; William Powell *(John Fletcher)*; Henry Stephenson *(Colonel Colby)*; Lilian

Powell and Harding outside the theater. *(Double Harness)*

Powell and Harding settle down for a serious talk. *(Double Harness)*

Henry Stephenson in a warm moment with Powell and Harding. *(Double Harness)*

A pleasant moment at luncheon for Powell and Harding, as Lilian Bond looks on. *(Double Harness)*

Bond *(Monica Page);* George Meeker *(Dennis);* Lucile Brown *(Valerie Colby);* Reginald Owen (Butler); Kay Hammond *(Eleanor Weston);* Leigh Allen *(Leonard Weston).*

CREDITS:

John Cromwell (Director); Kenneth Macgowan (Associate Producer); Jane Murfin (Screenplay); based on the play by Edward Poor Montgomery.

Running time, 82 minutes. Released July 1933.

ESSAY

The lovely and accomplished Ann Harding, then a top star at RKO, got Powell on loan for this from Warners in 1933. It was a polished drawing room comedy, and was literate as all-get-out. The Jane Murfin screenplay, from a play by Edward Poor Montgomery, had to do with a woman who gets a man to marry her via trickery, then is forced to earn his love honestly. Powell and Harding got all this across with considerable finesse, and the rather sparse plot was compensated by the fine acting and the fine direction by John Cromwell.

Given the dearth of plot, Jane Murfin was

Harding and Powell get serious. (*Double Harness*)

forced to flesh out the situations and cinematize them, which she proceeded to do with her usual expertise. Ann Harding gave one of her more sincere performances, and her chemistry meshed well with Powell's, so much so that a number of fans wrote in to ask why they weren't reunited for a subsequent picture. But that was not to be.

The critics welcomed the Harding-Powell combine, with one writing: "It has long been a source of wonderment to me as to why these two fine stage veterans, Ann Harding and William Powell, have not blended their seasoned talent and sparkingly individualistic personalities long before this." And from another: "There isn't that much plot—how do you make a marriage with an initially shaky foundation work? seems to be the basic premise. But Mr. Powell and Miss Harding give the doings—such as they are—a lot of personality and star-power. Things tend to get mighty talky, as they do in drawing-room stuff like this, but when two past masters of the spoken English word are doing thè talking, who would be so ungracious as to complain?"

Powell said in several 1933 magazine interviews that he had known Ann Harding during their stage years, back in the early 1920's, and had a solid respect for her talent. The respect was mutual, as Harding later revealed.

THE KENNEL MURDER CASE

1933 WARNER BROS.

CAST:

William Powell *(Philo Vance)*; Mary Astor *(Hilda Lake)*; Eugene Pallette *(Sergeant Heath)*; Ralph Morgan *(Raymond Wrede)*; Helen Vinson *(Doris Delafield)*; Jack La Rue *(Eduardo)*; Paul Cavanaugh *(Sir Thomas MacDonald)*; Robert Barrat *(Archer Coe)*; Arthur Hohl *(Gamble)*; Henry O'Neill *(Dubois)*; Frank Conroy *(Brisbane Coe)*.

CREDITS:

Michael Curtiz (Director); Robert Presnell (Supervisor); Robert Presnell (Screenplay); adapted from the novel *The Return of Philo Vance* by S. S. Van Dine.

Running time, 73 minutes. Released November 1933.

ESSAY

With the boxoffice plummeting during the 1932-33 period, Warners in 1933 decided to give their expensive star, Powell, yet another whirl with the Philo Vance character for his fourth Vance go-round (his first since 1930) in *The Kennel Murder Case.* While camera and directorial fluidity were greater in 1933 than in 1930, the photography more smooth and glistening, the story of *Kennel Murder Case* was no better and no worse than that of its predecessors, and some critics suggested that as of that point, the Philo Vance character, however charming and expert, had (for the time being, anyway) had his day.

In this story, based on the S. S. Van Dine novel, *The Return of Philo Vance,* a Doberman Pinscher, a most compelling example of the breed, figures heavily in the plot, as a collector of *chinoiserie* is murdered and a list of fascinating suspects is lined up for Vance's analysis, including Mary Astor as the niece of the deceased, Jack LaRue, Paul Cavanagh, Robert Barrat and Arthur Hohl, the last three looking suspicious enough for multiple murders, let alone one.

Mary Astor, who was later to enjoy considerably more fame at Warners via *The Maltese Falcon* and *The Great Lie* (both 1941), recalls working with Powell as a stimulating experience. Certainly their chemistries tallied better than his did with Bette Davis later in the year.

Eugene Pallette again played the slow-witted police sergeant, recalling to fans pleasantly his earlier renditions of the role, and the Doberman Pinscher proves an invaluable aide to Vance in ferreting out the murderer. Michael Curtiz was the right director for this,

Powell checking out the crime scene via miniatures. *(The Kennel Murder Case)*

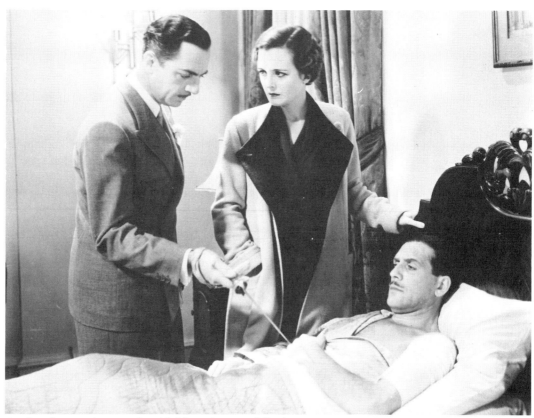

Getting down to brass tacks with Mary Astor and Paul Cavanagh. *(The Kennel Murder Case)*

149

Astor and Paul Cavanagh get an earful from Powell. (*The Kennel Murder Case*)

Eugene Pallette and Powell let Jack LaRue and Helen Vinson talk it over. (*The Kennel Murder Case*)

keeping the pace fast and the performances sleek—not that the experienced Powell needed any help from Curtiz with a role he had long since made his own.

"William Powell is expert as ever as Philo Vance, and the production values are smooth," one critic wrote, "but can't Warners come up with some new and original material for this talented star? Why keep him in reprise-stuff."

Is Helen Vinson telling Pallette and Powell what they want to know? (*The Kennel Murder Case*)

150

FASHIONS OF 1934

1934 WARNER BROS.

CAST:

William Powell *(Sherwood Nash);* Bette Davis *(Lynn Mason);* Frank McHugh *(Snap);* Hugh Herbert *(Joe Ward);* Phillip Reed *(Jimmy Blake);* Verree Teasdale *(The Duchess);* Reginald Owen *(Baroque).*

CREDITS:

William Dieterle (Director); Henry Blanke (Producer); F. Hugh Herbert, Gene Markey, Kathryn

Powell has news for Bette Davis and Phillip Reed.
(Fashions of 1934)

Scola and Carl Erickson (Screenplay); based on an original story by Harry Collins and Warren Duff; William Rees (Photographer); Dances by Busby Berkeley; Jack Killifer (Editor).

Running time, 78 minutes. Released January 1934.

ESSAY

In one of his final pictures for Warners, Powell found himself cast for the one and only time opposite Bette Davis, and a strange pair they made. Davis's popeyed intensity and constant moving contrasted oddly with Powell's laid-back style and smooth underplaying. The story was neither fish nor fowl nor good red-herring, obviously unable to make up its mind whether it was a Busby Berkeley musical extravaganza or a silly amusing tale of fashion-pirating in New York and Paris.

As one commentator later remarked, "[Berkeley] staged a finale in which fifty beautiful girls, clad in ostrich plumes, formed themselves into human harps, and then into a sixty-foot long feathered galleon with fans taking the place of oars."

When I saw this film several years ago at

Powell and Verree Teasdale get convivial. *(Fashions of 1934)*

Davis and Powell in a quiet moment. *(Fashions of 1934)*

Theatre 80 St. Marks in New York, the audience couldn't seem to make up its mind whether to laugh or gasp in awe at some of the elaborate Berkeley numbers, to say nothing of a fashion show sequence featuring styles so outlandish (by 1980's standards) as to be stupefying. Stupefying, too, was Bette Davis, so made-up, hatted and gowned as to be almost unrecognizable as the Bette Davis people usually paid to see, nor did her scenes with Powell strike sparks—a clear case of wrong chemistry which the studio bosses should have had the foresight to recognize.

The story, a rickety affair at best, courtesy of F. Hugh Herbert and Carl Erickson from a story by Harry Collins and Warren Duff, has Powell a sharp couturier from the canyons of Manhattan who goes to Paris with his secretary Davis (who also happens to be a model, hence the clothes she sports), to steal the fashion inspirations of French couturier Reginald Owen. The assorted adventures of the pair lead to some ups and some downs, mostly ups. Frank McHugh is amusing as a photo assistant who takes sneak pictures of styles

153

Davis and Powell have some "bar" talk. *(Fashions of 1934)*

from a miniature camera atop his cane, and Verree Teasdale is a "Russian Grand Duchess" who turns out *not* to be within hailing distance of the nobility. There were some songs thrown in, too, and William Dieterle kept the faintly vulgar doings sharply twirling.

THE KEY

1934   WARNER BROS.

CAST:

William Powell *(Captain Tennant);* Edna Best *(Norah Kerr);* Colin Clive *(Andrew Kerr);* Hobart Cavanaugh *(Homer);* Halliwell Hobbes *(The General);* Henry O'Neill *(Dan);* Phil Regan *(Young Irishman);* Donald Crisp *(Conlan);* J. M. Kerrigan *(O'Duffy);* Arthur Treacher *(Lieutenant Merriman).*

CREDITS:

Michael Curtiz (Director); Robert Presnell (Supervisor); Laird Doyle (Screenplay); based on the play by R. Gore-Brown and J. L. Hardy; Song: "There's a Cottage in Killarney" by Mort Dixon and Allie Wrubel.

Running time, 73 minutes. Released May 1934.

ESSAY

The Key was a picture that reportedly was one of Powell's favorites from his Warners era. Again he had Michael Curtiz as director, and Curtiz really delivered for him in this, his final Warners release before going to Metro-Goldwyn-Mayer and an even higher order of fame.

The plot was a more interesting one in quality terms than those usually allotted Powell in his Warners period. Based on a well-

Powell makes a dashing British officer.

Powell shows interest in Clive's wife, Edna Best. *(The Key)*

Colin Clive, director Michael Curtiz and Powell on the set. *(The Key)*

written screenplay by Laird Doyle from a play by R. Gore-Brown and J. L. Hardy, *The Key* displayed Powell as a British Army officer in the Ireland of 1920, a year of rebellion against the British, who is having a love affair with Edna Best, whose husband, Colin Clive, is in British intelligence.

In the course of a convoluted plot that highlights the difficulties between the Irish and English that eventually led to Irish independence (at least in the South), Powell, a brave officer whose Achilles' heel is his penchant for other men's wives, matures into a responsible, caring person. Edna Best is most eloquent and touching as Clive's wife, with whom Powell is in love, and Clive is his usual intense self as a man put upon from various directions, romantic and political.

Curtiz and the Warners art department tellingly caught the atmosphere of the Ireland of 1920, with the settings and general ambience uncannily right for an effort that never got out of Burbank, site of the Warner studio and back lots. Donald Crisp, J. M. Kerrigan and Arthur Treacher offered fine characterizations in support, with Crisp particularly fine.

156

A serious moment between Edna Best and Powell. *(The Key)*

Anne Shirley (then known as Dawn O'Day), sells flowers to Powell while Hobart Cavanaugh looks on. *(The Key)*

The Key had elements in it that anticipated John Ford's famous film *The Informer,* released the next year, 1935, and while *The Key* emphasized romance and melodrama primarily, it did get across more than a few intimations of Ireland's agony as it sought to throw off the yoke of Britain, once and for all. The reviewers were for the most part respectful, citing Powell's, Best's and Clive's fine performances and Curtiz's careful direction.

MANHATTAN MELODRAMA

1934 METRO-GOLDWYN-MAYER

A typical bit of Loy-Powell badinage with a hamburger. (*Manhattan Melodrama*)

Powell found Gable and Loy exciting new co-stars. (*Manhattan Melodrama*)

CAST:

Clark Gable (*Blackie Gallagher*); William Powell (*Jim Wade*); Myrna Loy (*Eleanor*); Leo Carrillo (*Father Pat*); Nat Pendleton (*Spud*); George Sidney (*Poppa Rosen*); Isabel Jewell (*Annabelle*); Muriel Evans (*May*); Claudelle Kay (*Miss Adams*); Frank Conroy (*Blackie's Attorney*); Jimmy Butler (*Jim as a boy*); Mickey Rooney (*Blackie as a boy*); Harry Seymour (*Pianist*); Landers Stevens (*Police Inspector*); Thomas Jackson (*Snow*); John Marston (*Coates*); Samuel S. Hinds (*Warden*); William Stack (*Judge*).

CREDITS:

W. S. Van Dyke II (Director); David O. Selznick (Producer); Oliver T. Marsh, H. P. Garrett, Joseph L. Mankiewicz (Screenplay); from a story by Ar-

thur Caesar; Joseph Wright, Edwin B. Willis (Art Directors); James Wong Howe (Photographer).

Running time, 93 minutes. Released May 1934

ESSAY

Powell scored heavily in his first picture for Metro-Goldwyn-Mayer, *Manhattan Melodrama.* In it he was aided and abetted by two power-house co-stars, Clark Gable and Myrna Loy; with both he was appearing for the first time. This marked the first of his pairings (from 1934 to 1947) with Myrna Loy—a combination that went over big with the fans and won them permanent renown as one of the greatest of screen teams.

Many years later, Myrna Loy recalled: "From the very first scene we did together in *Manhattan Melodrama,* we felt that particular magic there was between us. There was this feeling of rhythm, of complete understanding, and an instinct of how each of us could bring out the best in the other."

Powell, in the 1940's, took a stab at analyzing the magic between him and Loy—a chemistry so potent that it enthralled millions of fans. "She seemed to have an instinctive understanding of my moods and my technique;

Priest Leo Carrillo gets a warm reception from Loy and Powell.
(Manhattan Melodrama)

Sympathetic Loy comforts Powell as he decides on
friend Gable's fate. *(Manhattan Melodrama)*

160

Carrillo looks on as old friends Powell and Gable say a final goodbye. *(Manhattan Melodrama)*

she made them mesh with her own. We also shared a similar sense of humor. Myrna was a real pro; all of her moves were well thought out. It was an asset to my career to work with her."

Powell and Gable also got on well, though their styles were very different, and Gable knew Powell to be the more finished actor. The contrast in their mystiques worked out particularly well for this poignant story, which was well-paced by director Woody Van Dyke, who packed a lot of concentrated action and emotion into 93 minutes.

Powell and Gable are two friends who in childhood lose their parents in the *General Slocum* excursion-boat fire of 1904; this causes them to cling together. As they mature, the Powell character trods the straight and narrow, electing for the law and becoming district attorney in New York. Gable's character, a more free-wheeling, hedonistic type, turns to crime. Loy loves first Gable, then Powell, as she comes to realize the latter's intrinsic worth. Gable kills a man to protect Powell's good name, and when he becomes governor, Powell has the bitter duty of sending his friend to the electric chair, though he knows he killed the man for his sake. Loy, at first horrified at what she thinks is Powell's callousness (she has married him), returns to him when he publicly resigns, feeling he almost let friendship interfere with his duty.

THE THIN MAN

1934 METRO-GOLDWYN-MAYER

CAST:

William Powell *(Nick Charles)*; Myrna Loy *(Nora Charles)*; Maureen O'Sullivan *(Dorothy)*; Nat Pendleton *(Lieutenant John Guild)*; Minna Gombell *(Mimi Wynant)*; Porter Hall *(McCauley)*; Henry Wadsworth *(Tommy)*; William Henry *(Gilbert Wynant)*; Harold Huber *(Nunheim)*; Cesar Romero *(Chris Jorgenson)*; Natalie Moorhead *(Julia Wolf)*;

One of the famed Powell-Loy clinches. *(The Thin Man)*

Porter Hall and Minna Gombell seem to have Powell and Loy confused. *(The Thin Man)*

With their famous co-star Asta. *(The Thin Man)*

Edward Brophy *(Joe Morelli);* Clay Clement *(Quinn);* Thomas Jackson *(Reporter);* Walter Long *(Stutsy Burke);* Bert Roach *(Foster);* Ben Taggart *(Police Captain).*

CREDITS:

W. S. Van Dyke II (Director); Hunt Stromberg (Producer); Albert Hackett, Frances Goodrich (Screenplay); based on the Novel by Dashiell Hammett; Les Selander (Assistant Director); James Wong Howe (Photographer); Cedric Gibbons, David Townsend (Art Directors); Robert J. Kern (Editor).

Running time, 91 minutes. Released June 1934.

ESSAY

The Thin Man was the film that established Powell and Loy as one of the leading screen teams. It established Loy in the public mind as "The Perfect Wife" and presented Powell as the archetype of the jaunty, polished, humorous, sharp-witted and free-wheeling detective, as envisioned by Dashiell Hammett. Loy has recalled that "Nick and Nora" were a devoted couple in the modern, sophisticated style, loving each other in spite of their respective faults, seeking occasions for humor and fun wherever they went, turning the solving even

"Ice, anyone?" Powell seems to be saying to the telephoning Loy. *(The Thin Man)*

Powell kibitzes on Loy's discussion with Thomas Jackson. *(The Thin Man)*

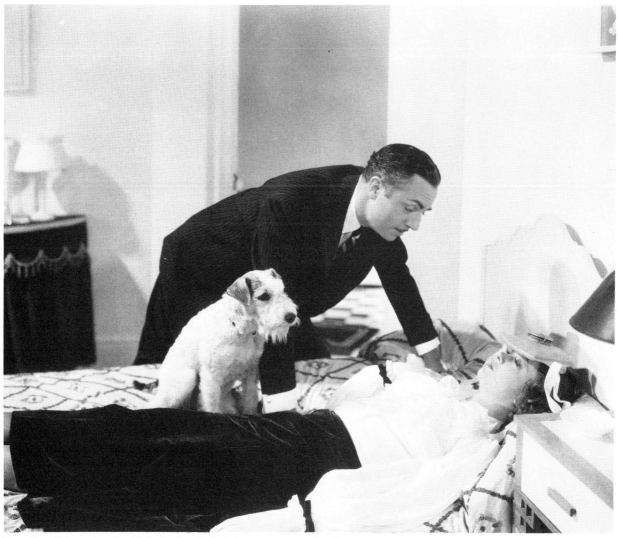

Powell and Asta wonder if the icebag is helping Loy any. *(The Thin Man)*

of murder mysteries into a wry, enchanting game of wits—with each other and with the murderer. They knew how to laugh *at* and *with* each other interchangeably, and they put into their roles a human, fresh, multi-dimensional quality that had not been seen on the screen before, and which stamped them as originals.

Shot in only twelve days by the famous "Woody-One-Take" Van Dyke, the film moved smoothly and fluidly, with Nick and Nora alternating good times on the town with some of the sharpest, freshest detective work on the screen. Albert Hackett and Frances Goodrich, that screenwriting powerhouse, caught all the nuances of the original—the sharp dialogue,

the tricky situations with their surprise twists, and the joyful hedonism of the Powell-Loy combine. The actual thin man, of course, was played by the angular Edward Ellis, an inventor who has disappeared. After his secretary is murdered, Powell's Nick Charles, aided by his wire-haired terrier, Asta, checks out the inventor's workshop, with the missing man at first under suspicion.

A cast of characters including Minna Gombell, Porter Hall, Henry Wadsworth and Natalie Moorhead provide all kinds of red-herring twists, but eventually it turns out that a dishonest lawyer killed Ellis when he was discovered by the victim mishandling his funds. But what gives this trailblazing film its utter

Loy is reading at bedtime but Powell has other ideas. *(The Thin Man)*

Some quiet Powell cordiality with Maureen O'Sullivan and Henry Wadsworth. *(The Thin Man)*

Gombell and O'Sullivan confer while Powell and Loy look on. *(The Thin Man)*

distinction and consummate individuality is the wonderful performing of Powell and Loy, who were given their head by Van Dyke.

EVELYN PRENTICE

1934 METRO-GOLDWYN-MAYER

CAST:

William Powell *(John Prentice)*; Myrna Loy *(Evelyn Prentice)*; Una Merkel *(Amy)*; Harvey Stephens *(Lawrence Kennard)*; Isabel Jewell *(Judith Wilson)*; Rosalind Russell *(Nancy Harrison)*; Henry Wadsworth *(Chester Wylie)*; Edward Brophy *(Eddie Delaney)*; Cora Sue Collins *(Dorothy)*; Jessie Ralph *(Mrs. Blake)*; Pat O'Malley *(Detective Thompson)*; Jack Mulhall *(Gregory)*; Herman Bing *(Antique Dealer)*; Samuel S. Hinds *(Newton)*; Howard Hickman *(Mr. Whitlock)*; Stanley Andrews *(Judge)*.

Powell and Loy seem lost in each other. *(Evelyn Prentice)*

CREDITS:

William K. Howard (Director); John W. Considine, Jr. (Producer); Lenore Coffee (Screenplay); based on the novel by W. E. Woodward; Charles G. Clarke (Photographer); Cedric Gibbons, Arnold Gillespie, Edwin B. Willis (Art Directors); Frank Hull (Editor).

Running time, 80 minutes. Released November 1934.

ESSAY

In their third time out, Powell and Loy found themselves again involved with criminal doings, though not as Nick and Nora. The proceedings this time were more solemn, with less opportunity for fey humor and amusing sallies, the prevailing mood being somber.

Evelyn Prentice, however, did demonstrate what needed no demonstrating—that Powell and Loy could enthrall audiences in a serious drama. Here Loy is the mother of Cora Sue

Danger threatens, but they have each other. *(Evelyn Prentice)*

A loving moment with their daughter, Cora Sue Collins. *(Evelyn Prentice)*

Does Loy want to tell Powell the truth here? *(Evelyn Prentice)*

Collins and the wife of busy trial-lawyer Powell, who has been defending client Rosalind Russell (it was her first picture) on a manslaughter rap. When Powell gets Russell acquitted, Loy suspects he is romancing her, which causes her to go tit-for-tat with writer Harvey Stephens.

Stephens turns out to be a blackmailer and Loy is given to believe that she has killed him during a scene at his apartment. She evades detection, however, and has to look on guiltily as Stephens' castoff girlfriend, Isabel Jewell, is put on trial. During a climactic moment in the courtroom, Loy cries out what she feels to be her own guilt, but a shocked Powell, determined to get to the bottom of the matter, eventually proves that Jewell was the murderer.

William K. Howard directed with an expert eye for the tensions implicit in the drama, and the Lenore Coffee screenplay helped Howard put a lot of narrative punch into the film. A strong supporting cast included Una Merkel, Edward Brophy and Jessie Ralph.

Powell turned in a performance of considerable dignity in this film, getting across the character of a seriously dedicated man of the law who pays a price for sacrificing his personal life with his wife and child to the exigencies of his career.

170

Are they having a moment of truth here? *(Evelyn Prentice)*

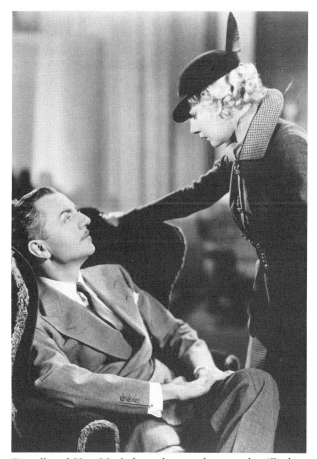

Powell and Una Merkel get down to brass tacks. *(Evelyn Prentice)*

Loy contemplates husband Powell. *(Evelyn Prentice)*

"Mr. Powell is most authoritative and characterizationally expert in his role," one critic noted," reminding us that he is an excellent actor in serious roles. He and Miss Loy play expertly together in a solidly scripted drama."

STAR OF MIDNIGHT

1935 RKO-RADIO

CAST:

William Powell *(Clay Dalzell)*; Ginger Rogers *(Donna Mantin)*; Paul Kelly *(Kinland)*; Gene Lockhart *(Swayne)*; Ralph Morgan *(Classon)*; Leslie Fenton *(Tim Winthrop)*; J. Farrell MacDonald *(Doremus)*; Russell Hopton *(Tommy Tennant)*; Frank Reicher *(Abe Ohlman)*.

CREDITS:

Stephen Roberts (Director); Howard J. Green, Anthony Veiller and Edward Kaufman (Screenplay); based on a novel by Arthur Somers Roche; Pandro S. Berman (Producer); J. Roy Hunt (Photogra-

Rogers and Powell talk it over at cocktail time. *(Star of Midnight)*

Powell gives Ralph Morgan a wryly speculative look during a confab with Rogers. *(Star of Midnight)*

pher); Max Steiner (Music); Arthur Roberts (Editor).

Running time, 90 minutes. Released April 1935.

ESSAY

Powell went on loan to RKO in 1935, and found himself playing a character named Clay Dalzell (the same number of letters as in Nick Charles), who resembled the playboy-detective of *The Thin Man*, the previous year's smash hit, perhaps more closely than his home studio, MGM, would have wished. It seems that a notorious gossipist has been murdered, and wealthy lawyer Powell is the chief suspect—on purely circumstantial evidence, of course. So he sets out to find the real murderer and prove himself innocent.

His distaff sidekick this time was Ginger Rogers, already a prominent RKO star thanks largely to her singing-dancing outings with Fred Astaire in their famed musicals. Here

Powell wonders what Rogers has in her purse during a hasty meal. (*Star of Midnight*)

she was taking a sabbatical from Astaire in order to enhance her fresh new stardom via osmosis with Powell.

An amusing, witty screenplay by the triple-threat team of Anthony Veiller-Howard J. Green-Edward Kaufman, based on a novel by Arthur Somers Roche, got fast-paced, classy treatment at the hands of director Stephen Roberts, and while the Powell-Rogers combine did not threaten to dim memories of the Powell-Loy duo or even the Powell-Francis pairing of several years past, they made a sparkling couple with a good mutual chemistry and an instinctive ability to keep the conversational tennis ball whacking back and forth via scintillating dialogue.

Meanwhile, both the cops and the underworld are giving Powell a hard time as he seeks to uncover the homicidal culprit and metamorphose himself from suspect to innocent man, and Rogers is there to render moral and other kinds of support when called upon.

The critics jumped on the similarity to the *Thin Man* series to a perhaps excessive degree, and some of them wondered why RKO, with MGM's valuable star on an inexplicable loan-out to them, had been allowed by the latter

J. Farrell MacDonald and Leslie Fenton hold the Powell-Rogers interest. (*Star of Midnight*)

studio to "get away with" what amounted to a reprise on the idea. But the public liked it, and even the critics, after getting "Thin Man" comparisons out of their respective systems, dubbed *Star of Midnight* "delightful," "fast-paced" and "witty."

An argument looms between Powell and Harlow. (*Reckless*)

RECKLESS

1935 METRO-GOLDWYN-MAYER

CAST:

Jean Harlow *(Mona Leslie)*; William Powell *(Ned Riley)*; Franchot Tone *(Bob Harrison)*; May Robson *(Granny)*; Ted Healy *(Smiley)*; Nat Pendleton *(Blossom)*; Robert Light *(Paul Mercer)*; Rosalind Russell *(Jo)*; Henry Stephenson *(Mr. Harrison)*; Louise

Harlow realizes that Powell loves her truly. *(Reckless)*

Henry *(Henry)*; James Ellison *(Dale Every)*; Leon Ames *(Ralph Watson)*; Man Mountain Dean *(Himself)*; Farina *(Gold Dust)*; Allan Jones *(Allan)*; Nina Mae McKinney and Carl Randell *(Themselves)*.

CREDITS:

Victor Fleming (Director); David O. Selznick (Producer); P. J. Wolfson (Screenplay); from an original story by Oliver Jeffries; George Folsey (Photographer); Margaret Booth (Editor); Songs by Jerome Kern and Oscar Hammerstein II.

Running time, 96 minutes. Released April 1935.

ESSAY

For his first picture with Jean Harlow, with whom he was by then carrying on a romance, Powell was assigned *Reckless*, a racy story about a Broadway star who marries an aristocrat who regrets the marriage and later kills himself. Powell plays the man who loves Harlow in secret and finally wins her for his own, after the scandal has almost ruined her career. As the Broadway Baby, Harlow's singing was dubbed and a double did her dancing

Tone resists the Harlow-Powell efforts to calm him down. *(Reckless)*

May Robson congratulates Harlow and Tone on their wedding while Powell looks glum. *(Reckless)*

A Powell-Harlow studio glamor pose. *(Reckless)*

for her, nevertheless MGM implied in its ads that Harlow demonstrated, in *Reckless*, triple-threat talents along those respective lines.

Harlow was angry with MGM for being forced to do the picture, which seemed not only to be tastelessly capitalizing on the suicide, under mysterious circumstances, of her second husband, producer Paul Bern, in 1932, but also evoked memories of the suicide of Broadway singer Libby Holman's young husband, tobacco heir Zachary Reynolds, the same year as Bern died. Powell persuaded her that to refuse to do the film would only result in a suspension and further adverse publicity, so she went ahead with it, reluctantly. Victor Fleming directed.

Seen fifty years later at Frank Rowley's Regency Theatre in New York, *Reckless* has not held up well, seeming poorly constructed and with carelessly motivated characterizations. The reviews of 1935 were not sensational either, with more than one reviewer considering it a cheap, shoddy exploitational film that fed on the tragedies of two well-known personalities. Harlow tries hard to improve her acting in this, but her tension and inner strain are apparent in several scenes (and who could blame her, considering the autobiographical nuances and overtones insinuated by the screenwriters).

Powell is strictly along for support of Jean's sometimes volatile, sometimes flagging spirits; he is required to carry a torch when Harlow marries Franchot Tone, to be supportive in her time of trial, and to be on hand to win her at the finish, which comes at the end of a rather flashy and vulgar musical in which Harlow has forced the gossipy, malicious audience to accept her, appealing as she does to their "sportsmanship," if that is the term for it. The Powell-Harlow offscreen chemistry was not much in evidence *on*-screen in this, the first of the two MGM films they would do together.

Powell freezes out the importunate Frank Morgan for a dance with Rainer. (*Escapade*)

Powell and May Robson consider Harlow's plight. (*Reckless*)

ESCAPADE

1935 METRO-GOLDWYN-MAYER

CAST:

William Powell *(Fritz);* Luise Rainer *(Leopoldina);* Frank Morgan *(Karl);* Virginia Bruce *(Gerta);* Reginald Owen *(Paul);* Mady Christians *(Anita);* Laura Hope Crews *(Countess);* Henry Travers *(Concierge);* Mathilda Coment *(Carmen).*

CREDITS:

Robert Z. Leonard (Director); Bernard Hyman (Producer); Herman Mankiewicz (Screenplay); based on the play by Walter Reisch and the German film, *Maskerade;* Bronislau Kaper and Walter Jurmann (Musical Score); Gus Kahn and Harold Adamson (Lyrics).

Running time, 92 minutes. Released July 1935.

Powell and Virginia Bruce in a tête-à-tête. *(Escapade)*

Mathilde Comont consoles Powell. *(Escapade)*

ESSAY

When Myrna Loy left for Europe after informing Louis B. Mayer that she would do no more work without the kind of money she felt her box office status warranted, Mayer was forced to cast new actresses in parts that had been tailored to the Loy talents. One of these actresses was newcomer Luise Rainer, from Vienna, whose fabulous talent was immediately recognized by Powell, who plumped for her after he found her cast in his new picture in place of Loy. Later he was so impressed with her highly individual and sparkling performance in *Escapade* that he even made a trailer for the studio introducing her and demanded that she be given co-starring status with him above the picture's title.

Escapade itself was a slight affair, strong on atmosphere and acting turns but short on plot, about an artist in Vienna (Powell) with a compulsion to dally with all the lovely ladies he can ferret out. On hand for his assorted romancings are such as Virginia Bruce and Mady Christians, and in sterling support can be found those character heavyweights Laura Hope Crews, Frank Morgan, Reginald Owen and Henry Travers.

Robert Z. Leonard did what he could with what scenarist Herman Mankiewicz provided, based on a Walter Reisch comedy about pre-war Vienna and its obsession with (preferably light and fleeting) romance. *Escapade* was a remake of a German film, *Maskerade*, that had been a hit in Europe the year before.

In one of the most glamorous film roles he was ever to have, the 43-year-old Powell shone with masculine charisma, glorying in his con-

quests as he sows wild oats all over the Austrian capital. Of course when he meets the lovely Rainer, things get more serious than usual. How he deals with Rainer—and how she deals with him—constitutes an attraction-repulsion duel of the sexes of a more scintillating kind, and audiences and critics ate it up.

"Powell in one of his more glamorous romantic roles; a lovely new star, Luise Rainer, with a distinctively fey persona, glamorous settings, a lavish production—what more can Hollywood possibly offer?" one critic enthused.

Mady Christians likes what Powell is telling her. (*Escapade*)

Mathilde Comont cries for a sympathetic Powell. *(Escapade)*

Virginia Bruce knows she has Powell hooked—
for a time. *(Escapade)*

180

RENDEZVOUS

1935 METRO-GOLDWYN-MAYER

CAST:

William Powell (Bill Gordon); Rosalind Russell (Joel); Binnie Barnes (Olivia); Lionel Atwill (William Brennan); Cesar Romero (Nickolajeff); Samuel S. Hinds (Carter); Henry Stephenson (Ambassador); Frank Reicher (Dr. Jackson); Charles Grapewin (Martin).

CREDITS:

William K. Howard (Director): Lawrence Weingarten (Producer); Bella and Samuel Spewack, P. J. Wolfson and George Oppenheimer (Screenplay); based on *The American Black Chamber* (non-fiction) by Major H. O. Yardley.

Running time, 91 minutes. Released November 1935.

ESSAYS

Along with Luise Rainer, Rosalind Russell, who had been recruited from the Broadway stage and was demonstrating increasing appeal and expertise on the screen, profited from Myrna Loy's strike for more MGM money and found herself in a co-starring spot with Powell in *Rendezvous*.

Directed by William K. Howard, from a screenplay based on the non-fiction book *The American Black Chamber*, by Major H. O. Yardley, *Rendezvous* had to do with skullduggery involving a German spy ring in the Washington of 1917. Powell plays a cryptographer and Russell is a bubble-headed socialite who blunders and bumbles between Powell, the spies (Binnie Barnes and Cesar Romero)

Powell seems alarmed by his juxtaposition to Russell. (*Rendezvous*)

Powell and Samuel S. Hinds find dizzy Russell no help in their deliberations. (*Rendezvous*)

Barnes watches while Powell and Russell interact. (*Rendezvous*)

Spy Binnie Barnes cats-and-mouses it with Powell. (*Rendezvous*)

and all of Washington officialdom, almost bringing on the German spies' triumph *uber alles* before the whole business is finally set right by Powell and company.

The spy stuff is leavened with some refreshing humor, and Powell and Russell are delightful together, with Russell, in her first starring role, demonstrating a nice feel for comedic nuances. A good supporting cast of Barnes, Romero, Lionel Atwill, Henry Stephenson and Samuel S. Hinds helped things along expertly.

While enjoying the spy suspense, most of the 1935 critics zeroed-in on the sudden and sparkling humorous touches in the clever screenplay concocted by Bella and Samuel

182

Spewack, P. J. Wolfson and George Oppenheimer, all dependable wordsmiths.

"William Powell, with a refreshingly comical and incidentally poised-and-lovely leading lady, the relative newcomer Rosalind Russell, gives us a triple dose of his usual suspense-and-humor skills, and the Powell-Russell exchanges elicited considerable glee from the audience," one reviewer noted.

And from another: "William Powell is a self-starter, and he could carry any picture on his own, so supremely talented and endlessly resourceful is he, but in this instance he has a new leading lady, Rosalind Russell, who plays off him superbly, and the result is freshly inspired entertainment."

THE GREAT ZIEGFELD

1936 METRO-GOLDWYN-MAYER

CAST:

William Powell *(Florenz Ziegfeld);* Luise Rainer *(Anna Held);* Myrna Loy *(Billie Burke);* Frank Morgan *(Billings);* Reginald Owen *(Sampston);* Nat Pendleton *(Sandow);* Virginia Bruce *(Audrey Lane);* Ernest Cossart *(Sidney);* Robert Greig *(Joe);* Raymond Walburn *(Sage);* Fannie Brice *(Herself);* Ann Pennington (Herself); Ray Bolger *(Himself);* Harriet Hoctor *(Herself);* A.A. Trimble *(Will Rogers);* Joan Holland *(Patricia Ziegfeld);* Buddy Doyle *(Eddie Cantor);* William Demarest *(Gene Buck).*

CREDITS:

Robert Z. Leonard (Director); Hunt Stromberg (Producer); William Anthony McGuire (Story and Screenplay); Cedric Gibbons (Art Director); Oliver T. Marsh, Ray June, George Folsey, Merritt B. Gerstad (Photographers); Adrian (Costumes); Arthur Lange (Music Director); Songs by Irving Berlin, Walter Donaldson and Harold Adamson; Douglas Shearer (Sound); William S. Gray (Editor).

Running time, 180 minutes. Released April 1936.

With his costars Rainer, Loy and Bruce. *(The Great Ziegfeld)*

Powell and Loy are en-
thralled by one of his
shows. *(The Great Ziegfeld)*

Powell finds marital happiness with Loy. *(The Great Ziegfeld)*

ESSAY

Powell was regarded as the perfect choice to play the legendary Florenz Ziegfeld, the consummate showman who in the 1907-32 period "glorified the American girl" in a series of Broadway entertainments that made him—and them—famous the world over. Billie Burke, Ziegfeld's widow and the charming actress who later made a whole new name for herself as one of the most sparkling character players on the screen, personally chose Powell for the role, claiming that while he didn't resemble her husband physically, he had the right manner and approach. She was right, for Ziegfeld turned out to be one of Powell's more acclaimed filmic incarnations.

Costing a phenomenal (by 1936 standards) million and a half dollars, the Robert Z. Leonard-directed extravaganza, which traced Ziegfeld's entire career, from his 1890's sponsorship of strong-man Sandow and his adventures at the 1893 Chicago World's Fair to his

Rainer catches Powell with Virginia Bruce. *(The Great Ziegfeld)*

It's tickle-time for Powell and Rainer. *(The Great Ziegfeld)*

initiation of the famed Follies in 1907, which led to the great career as a musical entrepreneur culminating in the 1927 *Show Boat*—followed by declining years and his death in 1932 at the bottom of the Depression.

Luise Rainer is on hand as the chanteuse Anna Held, Ziegfeld's first wife (Rainer won her first Oscar in this for a telephone scene in which she poignantly hid her grief while congratulating Powell on his second marriage, to Loy's Billie Burke), and while there was some criticism of Myrna Loy playing Billie Burke (the two actresses were very dissimilar in looks and temperament), there was some commendation for her poise and charm in the role.

Powell got across the poignancy implicit in Ziegfeld's financial misfortunes after the crash of 1929, and his love for his daughter Patricia is limned with sensitivity. Powell later said of his "Ziegfeld" role: "What I tried to do primarily was to get across the essential spirit of the man—his love for show business, his exquisite taste, his admiration for the beauty of women. He was financially impractical but

Virginia Bruce tells off Powell. (*The Great Ziegfeld*)

Powell admires Rainer's beauty. (*The Great Ziegfeld*)

Bruce gives Powell a hard time. *(The Great Ziegfeld)*

esthetically impeccable—a unique genius in his chosen field." The critics considered Powell "winning," "authoritative," "poised, charming and strangely touching" as Ziegfeld. He communicated the man's vulnerability of spirit as well as his special genius.

Powell, Loy and their screen daughter admire the dollhouse. *(The Great Ziegfeld)*

A quiet Powell-Loy moment. *(The Great Ziegfeld)*

With costars Rainer and Loy. *(The Great Ziegfeld)*

187

With the three lovely
leads of the picture. *(The
Great Ziegfeld)*

Powell cogitates while Arthur watches.
(The Ex-Mrs. Bradford)

THE EX-MRS. BRADFORD

1936 RKO-RADIO

CAST:

William Powell *(Dr. Bradford);* Jean Arthur *(Paula Bradford);* James Gleason *(Inspector Corrigan);* Eric Blore *(Stokes);* Robert Armstrong *(Mike);* Lila Lee *(Miss Prentiss);* Grant Mitchell *(Mr. Summers);* Erin O'Brien-Moore *(Mrs. Summers);* Ralph Morgan *(Mr. Hutchins);* Lucille Gleason *(Mrs. Hutchins).*

CREDITS:

Stephen Roberts (Director); Edward Kaufman (Associate Producer); Anthony Veiller (Screenplay); based on a story by James Edward Grant; J. Roy Hunt (Photographer); Roy Webb (Music Director); Arthur Roberts (Editor).

Running time, 80 minutes. Released May 1936.

ESSAY

Powell went through one of his periodic loanouts—this time again to RKO—for *The Ex-Mrs. Bradford*, in which he found himself cast with the delightful Jean Arthur, who was herself on loan from Columbia. Powell had fond memories of Arthur when she played with him in his early talkies, and the reunion was a happy one, all the more so because they knew they had a good script on hand, a director (Stephen Roberts) who understood the material, and some sterling supporting players, including Robert Armstrong, Ralph Morgan, Lila Lee and Grant Mitchell.

Powell had it in his MGM contract that he could not be loaned out without his okay, but he liked the script of *The Ex-Mrs. Bradford* and felt instinctively that it would be a hit that would enhance his bargaining power as a Metro-Goldwyn-Mayer star. His instinct was right, as the picture was well liked by critics and public.

Eric Blore and Powell engage in some champagne-bottle monkeyshines. (*The Ex-Mrs. Bradford*)

Powell, Arthur and James Gleason try to figure out the mystery. (*The Ex-Mrs. Bradford*)

Whatever Powell and Arthur are watching, it must be a riveting sight. (*The Ex-Mrs. Bradford*)

Of course it was yet another retread of the *Thin Man* theme (this had also been true of his 1935 loanout to RKO, *Star of Midnight*), but Powell felt that the fresh treatment and the chemistry with Jean Arthur would redeem the total.

189

The story involves a famous surgeon (Powell) whose ex-wife, Arthur, is constantly devising schemes to win him back. It seems that crime detection is the ex-Mrs. Bradford's hobby, and soon she involves Powell as chief suspect (in the mind of police inspector James Gleason) in a race track murder. Whereupon surgeon Powell turns sleuth and sets out to clear his name by solving the murders on his own, with Arthur making a nuisance of herself by offering tips and second-guessing the investigators on hand.

One critic wrote: "It's fearfully familiar ground, this man-woman sparring while a murder is being solved, and one would think there would be a danger of Mr. William Powell wearing out the genre. After all, how many twists and turns can one give such situations? But to our surprise, this gifted actor, ably abetted by the delightful Jean Arthur, makes it all seem fresh and novel. We went to the screening with misgivings; we are glad to be proven wrong."

Lombard begins to moon over a suspicious Powell. (*My Man Godfrey*)

MY MAN GODFREY

1936 UNIVERSAL

CAST:

William Powell (*Godfrey Parke*); Carole Lombard (*Irene Bullock*); Alice Brady (*Angelica Bullock*); Gail Patrick (*Cornelia Bullock*); Jean Dixon (*Molly*); Eugene Pallette (*Alexander Bullock*); Alan Mowbray (*Tommy Gray*); Mischa Auer (*Carlo*); Robert Light (*Faithful George*); Pat Flaherty (*Mike*); Franklin Pangborn (*Master of Ceremonies*); Grady Sutton (*Van Rumple*); Edward Gargan (*Detective*); James Flavin (*Detective*); Robert Perry (*Doorman*).

CREDITS:

Gregory LaCava (Director); Maurice Pivar (Supervisor); Morrie Ryskind and Eric Hatch (Screenplay); based on the novel by Eric Hatch; Ted Tetzlaff (Photographer); Charles Previn (Music); Charles D. Hall (Art Director); Ted Kent (Editor).

Gail Patrick tries to get snooty with Powell. (*My Man Godfrey*)

190

Running time, 93 minutes. Released September 1936.

ESSAY

Metro-Goldwyn-Mayer agreed to lend Powell to Universal for what turned out to be the screwball comedy hit of 1936—or any year. Gregory La Cava, that proven comic master, directed *My Man Godfrey,* and he made a comic masterpiece of it. Powell, wishing to put some adrenalin in the career fortunes of his ex-wife, Carole Lombard, who was limping along in only so-so pictures at that point,

Powell has a cure for what ails Alice Brady. *(My Man Godfrey)*

Lombard and Patrick have a discussion in front of Powell. *(My Man Godfrey)*

recommended to Universal that she play opposite him, resulting in a third Lombard-Powell teaming on the screen.

Powell always gave La Cava the major share of the credit for what resulted. As he later

191

related, "Every day he'd [La Cava] give us dialogue he'd written during the night before, and it was good dialogue. There never has been a man like Godfrey [the character Powell played] but La Cava made him seem really quite plausible."

The screenplay by Morrie Ryskind and Eric Hatch, based on a novel by Eric Hatch, was one of those items so popular during the Depression Thirties, in which the fortunes of the upper and lower classes are contrasted sharply. In this, Godfrey Parke is the scion of an old Boston family who has fallen upon hard times due to romantic troubles. Two debutantes, Lombard and her sister, Gail Patrick, discover him (Powell) while on a scavenger hunt to a shanty town in Manhattan inhabited by derelicts and Depression castaways. Soon, via Lombard's intrigued interest in him, he is serving as a man of all work at the mansion of her parents, Eugene Pallette and Alice Brady.

Promoted to butler, he is soon solving all the problems of this zany family which lives in the unreal, pixieish, totally impractical world of the rich. He puts snooty Patrick in her place, gets rid of bubble-head Brady's gigolo (Mischa Auer) and brings Lombard down to earth.

Wet-haired Lombard goes wild for Powell. *(My Man Godfrey)*

Powell and Lombard seem to be persuading the gentlemen of their position. *(My Man Godfrey)*

Later he helps his friends at Shantytown by building a nightclub nearby and wins Lombard in marriage.

The fun in *Godfrey* lay in La Cava's treatment of the material, with assorted debunkings, hilarious putdowns and tart sociological comment. It turned out to be the hit of the year, and set the standard for satirical screwball zaniness.

192

Powell loves Loy and Harlow loves Tracy. *(Libeled Lady)*

LIBELED LADY

1936 METRO-GOLDWYN-MAYER

CAST:

William Powell *(Bill Chandler)*; Myrna Loy *(Connie Allenbury)*; Jean Harlow *(Gladys Benton)*; Spencer Tracy *(Warren Haggerty)*; Walter Connolly *(James B. Allenbury)*; Charley Grapewin *(Hollis Bane)*; Cora Witherspoon *(Mrs. Burns-Norvell)*; E.E. Clive *(Evans)*; Charles Trowbridge *(Graham)*; Spencer Charters *(Magistrate)*; Greta Meyer *(Connie's Maid)*; Richard Tucker *(Barker)*; Hattie McDaniel *(Maid)*; Howard Hickman *(Cable Editor)*; Harry C. Bradley *(Justice of the Peace)*; Bodil Rosing *(Wife of Justice of the Peace)*.

Powell contemplates a beflowered Loy. *(Libeled Lady)*

A happy moment for a famous duo. (*Libeled Lady*)

CREDITS:

Jack Conway (Director); Lawrence Weingarten (Producer); Maurine Watkins, Howard Emmett Rogers, George Oppenheimer (Screenplay); based on a Story by Wallace Sullivan; Cedric Gibbons, William Hornung (Art Directors); Norbert Brodine (Photographer); Douglas Shearer (Sound); Dolly Tree (Wardrobe); Frederick Smith (Editor).

Running time, 98 minutes. Released November 1936.

ESSAY

Libeled Lady offered the powerhouse combination of Powell, Loy, Jean Harlow and Spencer Tracy in an amusing romantic mix-up expertly guided by director Jack Conway, with George Oppenheimer providing numerous laughlines and twist situations.

In the best traditions of screwball comedy, in 1936 quite the vogue, the story has newspaper editor Tracy running a story that involves heiress Loy with a married British peer whose wife screams her outrage to high heaven. Screaming libel (she had never been involved with the peer), Loy sues for millions. Though Tracy is about to marry Harlow, whom he has often stood up, to her exasperation, he comes up with the idea of marrying her off instead to Powell, an old friend, so that Powell can court Loy, then compromise her by getting "wife" Harlow to sue for alienation of affections. This is designed to cause Loy to shy off from the libel suit for fear of additional scandal.

The fun comes when Powell, courting Loy, has to convince her blustery father, Walter Connolly, that he can fish when he knows nothing about the sport. (Note: By luck, he catches the fish anyway.) Though initially suspicious of him, Loy gradually comes under Powell's spell. To his surprise, Powell finds that he returns her feeling. There are explanations all around, Harlow finally bags Tracy for her husband, and Powell and Loy are happily paired off, but not before a number of surprise twists are played out.

This was Powell's second filmic outing with Harlow, and much excitement was generated among the fans, since their romance was well-known in 1936. Tracy and Loy garnered fine reviews, as did their co-stars, with Tracy proving he was as expert a comedian as he was a dramatic actor.

Libeled Lady, seen in 1985 at Frank Rowley's Regency Revival Theatre in New York, proved as hypnotically amusing to a current audience as it was fifty years ago, garnering delighted chuckles throughout, and at times some noisy, but heartfelt, guffaws. The comedy situations, so expertly played, have a freshness and timelessness all their own.

Libeled Lady did well at the boxoffice, and garnered some fine reviews, with "amusing" and "winning" heading the list of critics' adjectives.

Powell sets out to impress the lady. *(Libeled Lady)*

195

It's fussin' time for Harlow and Tracy while the others look on ruefully.
(*Libeled Lady*)

Walter Connolly looks serious with Tracy while Powell and Loy wonder
what's up. (*Libeled Lady*)

AFTER THE THIN MAN

1936 METRO-GOLDWYN-MAYER

CAST:

William Powell *(Nick Charles);* Myrna Loy *(Nora Charles);* James Stewart *(David Graham);* Joseph Calleia *(Dancer);* Elissa Landi *(Selma Landis);* Jessie Ralph *(Aunt Katherine Forrest);* Alan Marshal *(Robert Landis);* Sam Levene *(Lieutenant Abrams);* Penny Singleton *(Polly Byrnes);* Dorothy Vaughn *(Charlotte);* Maude Turner Gordon *(Helen);* Teddy Hart *(Floyd Casper);* William Law *(Lum Kee);* George Zucco *(Doctor Adolph Kammer);* Paul Fix *(Phil Byrnes).*

CREDITS:

W.S. Van Dyke II (Director); Hunt Stromberg (Producer); Frances Goodrich, Albert Hackett (Screenplay); based on a Story by Dashiell Hammett; Oliver T. Marsh (Photographer); Songs by Arthur Freed and Nacio Herb Brown; Herbert Stothart (Music); Robert J. Kern (Editor).

Running time, 110 minutes. Released December 1936.

ESSAY

Due to the boxoffice potency of the original item in the *Thin Man* series (it was hailed as one of the Best Pictures of 1934), MGM decided to re-team Powell and Loy in a sequel, with W.S. Van Dyke again at the directorial helm.

The year 1936 had been a big one for Powell and Loy, with both appearing in one hit after another; Powell had to take second place to Loy in only one respect; she was named top feminine boxoffice star for 1936 by the nation's exhibitors, with Powell not far behind in the fans' esteem.

Again audiences loved Nick, Nora and Asta, who again carouse away the evenings, sleep all day, put each other on and exchange sharp

Asta looks the most poised of a poised threesome. *(After the Thin Man)*

197

Whatever the questions, this pair has the answers. *(After the Thin Man)*

Sam Levene questions Loy while Powell and Stewart look on.
(*After the Thin Man*)

Elissa Landi looks beyond comforting by Loy here, while Powell and Levene look helpless. (*After the Thin Man*)

wisecracks, with variations on Powell's twitting Loy that if she ever becomes a widow she won't be one for long—not with *her* money! Nick rouses himself from his partying, hedo-

It's morning-paper time but Levene and Powell won't let Loy read. (*After the Thin Man*)

George Zucco looks baleful while Powell and Loy puzzle things out. (*After the Thin Man*)

Will they never keep Asta's paws out of the icebox?
(*After the Thin Man*)

nistic life only when his sharp detective's mind senses an interesting crime mystery which, with his open contempt for the dumb police, he is sure he, and he alone, can solve.

Again there are a slew of suspects, with the usual closing gambit of rounding them all up in one room and, after the usual red-herring feintings, unmasking the murderer.

The typical convoluted murder plot has Elissa Landi (once a star, now on the way down via supporting roles) deputizing Nick to find her missing husband. The husband has been dallying with a singer whose former sweetheart, James Stewart, bribes Landi's husband, Alan Marshal, to disappear. Marshal, however, is murdered, and Landi and others are under suspicion. But the murderer turns out to be Stewart.

James Stewart, whose shy, winning manner and gangly awkwardness had already become the trademarks of his persona, is surprisingly convincing as the young man of homicidal bent, who had become unbalanced because Landi had rejected him originally to marry Marshal. Sam Levene is amusing as the police detective who gets his comeuppance from

Head to head, they look like they're planning some fun. (*After the Thin Man*)

Nick, and Jessie Ralph is among those lending sterling support. When Powell at the close registers astonishment because Loy is knitting a small garment, she snorts, "And you call yourself a detective!" Which sent the 1936 audience home in good humor.

The famed duo wax romantic here. *(After the Thin Man)*

THE LAST OF MRS. CHEYNEY

1937 METRO-GOLDWYN-MAYER

CAST:

Joan Crawford *(Mrs. Fay Cheyney)*; William Powell *(Charles)*; Robert Montgomery *(Lord Arthur)*; Frank Morgan *(Lord Kelton)*; Benita Hume *(Kitty)*; Aileen Pringle *(Maria)*; Ralph Forbes *(Cousin John)*; Jessie Ralph *(Duchess)*; Nigel Bruce *(Willie)*; Melville Cooper *(William)*; Sara Haden *(Anna)*; Lumsden Hare *(Inspector Witherspoon)*.

CREDITS:

Richard Boleslawski (Director); Lawrence Weingarten (Producer); Leon Gordon, Samson Raphaelson and Monckton Hoffe (Screenplay); based on the play *The Last of Mrs. Cheyney* by Frederick Lonsdale; George Folsey (Photographer); Cedric Gibbons (Art Director); Frank Sullivan (Editor).

Running time, 98 minutes. Released March 1937.

ESSAY

Someone got the idea of casting William Powell with Joan Crawford in a remake of the 1929 Norma Shearer vehicle, *The Last of Mrs. Cheyney*. It wasn't the happiest of inspirations, for the Crawford and Powell mystiques and/or chemistries mixed like the proverbial oil and water, and they never did another picture together. This was the rather off-target result of MGM's craze to pair its biggest male stars opposite its top feminine luminaries, feeling (sometimes mistakenly) that double star-power meant double boxoffice returns. The Powell-Crawford combination was one of their mistakes.

Robert Montgomery, whose stellar pres-

Powell tries to talk sense into a jaw-jutting Crawford. *(The Last of Mrs. Cheyney)*

Frank Morgan wants some explanations and Crawford hasn't any. Powell tries to bluff it out while Benita Hume, Ralph Forbes and Jessie Ralph, among others, puzzle it through. *(The Last of Mrs. Cheyney)*

Crawford looks grim while Powell and Montgomery talk it over. *(The Last of Mrs. Cheyney)*

A Montgomery-Crawford-Powell glamor pose.
(The Last of Mrs. Cheyney)

A calmer moment for the Powell-Crawford combination. *(The Last of Mrs. Cheyney)*

Lumsden Hare has bad news for the threesome. *(The Last of Mrs. Cheyney)*

ence was far more complementary to Crawford's (though they personally disliked each other), was the third member of what was hoped would be a triple-threat combination. Director Richard Boleslawski died as the film neared completion, and the rather dismal and

Powell and Crawford as elegant auctioneers. *(The Last of Mrs. Cheyney)*

trivial results indicated that he had been in terminally poor health during the shooting. Another element was that the Mrs. Cheyney saga was a tale told once too often, and the best efforts of another writing trio—Leon Gordon-Samson Raphaelson-Monckton Hoffe—couldn't get this humpty dumpty back on the wall.

The Frederick Lonsdale play on which this was based had been a Broadway hit back in the 1920's, and Shearer, in her first talkie year, had had a nice success with it; but by 1937 the threads were not only showing, but snapping, in this threadbare plot.

The story, such as it is (Lonsdale's play had depended on smart dialogue and clever performances to put it over) involves a jewel thief, Crawford, who poses as a lady while casing, and robbing, aristocratic establishments all over England. Powell is her confederate who poses as a butler, and Montgomery is a peer who gets Crawford to fall in love with him and who is instrumental in her "reform." Powell was very deft in his suave, slightly sinister impersonation, and acted rings around Crawford in a métier with which he had more familiarity professionally. Critics shrugged this one off. Frank Morgan, Benita Hume and Nigel Bruce, among others, did what they could to keep it afloat—but the leaks were too much for them.

THE EMPEROR'S CANDLESTICKS

1937 METRO-GOLDWYN-MAYER

CAST:

William Powell *(Baron Stephan Wolensky)*; Luise Rainer *(Countess Olga Mironova)*; Robert Young *(Grand Duke Peter)*; Maureen O'Sullivan *(Maria)*; Frank Morgan *(Colonel Baron Suroff)*; Henry Stephenson *(Prince Johan)*; Douglas Dumbrille *(Korum)*; Charles Waldron *(Doctor Malchor)*; Frank Reicher *(Pavloff)*.

It's intrigue time for Frank Conroy, Powell and Rainer. *(The Emperor's Candlesticks)*

Powell and Loy survey the crucial candlesticks. *(The Emperor's Candlesticks)*

CREDITS:

George Fitzmaurice (Director); John Considine, Jr. (Producer); Herman Mankiewicz, Monckton Hoffe and Harold Goldman (Screenplay); based on the story by Baroness Orczy; Hal Rosson (Photographer); Franz Waxman (Music.)

Running time, 89 minutes. Released July 1937.

ESSAY

The Baroness Orczy had written a popular tale of espionage in pre-World War I European capitals, and Metro-Goldwyn-Mayer decided it might make a nice glamor-showcase, replete with costumes and lavish settings, for the third teaming of William Powell and Luise Rainer, fresh from her Oscar-winner for their previous *The Great Ziegfeld*. George Fitzmaurice, the director, labored mightily to give the rather insubstantial doings some class and sizzle, and the screenplay that Herman Mankiewicz, Harold Goldman and Monckton Hoffe concocted from the by then creaky original aimed at showcasing Powell and Rainer in sparkling situations with sharply sophisticated dialogue, but the result was a rather insubstantial offering which found only passing favor with the public. The critics too were unimpressed, and while they found the star-teaming of Powell and Rainer welcome as usual, they deplored the trite and gossamer-thin plot.

Powell and Rainer find themselves in Russia as spies—on opposite sides. They go in for all kinds of intrigue, including the subterfuge which gives the film its title—they hide state secrets in a pair of candlesticks of museum quality, which are transported hither and thither. There are encounters with magistrates, rival inquisition teams and fellow espionage agents; there are handsome ballroom and drawing-room settings; and much scurrying around, but the total added up to a handsomely mounted mishmash, with only the stars' charisma to give it any sparkle.

In an able supporting cast, laboring overtime to give some substance to the story (so slight as to be almost non-existent) were such sterling players as Maureen O'Sullivan, Frank Morgan, Robert Young, Douglas Dumbrille, Henry Stephenson, E. E. Clive and Frank Conroy.

A typical review of 1937 put it on the line: "Powell and Rainer are a delightful stellar combination, but they need to be cast in more solid fare than this. The plot, what there is of it, creaks; a host of fine character players try to make something out of nothing; and splendid mounting and fine direction cannot successfully disguise the flimsiness of this soufflé conceit."

The pair try to outwit a police investigation here. (*The Emperor's Candlesticks*)

DOUBLE WEDDING

1937 METRO-GOLDWYN-MAYER

Powell is an artist with a yen for Loy. (*Double Wedding*)

CAST:

William Powell (*Charles Ledge*); Myrna Loy (*Margit Agnew*); John Beal (*Waldo Beaver*); Florence Rice (*Irene Agnew*); Jessie Ralph (*Mrs. Kensington Bly*); Edgar Kennedy (*Spike*); Sidney Toler (*Keogh*); Barnett Parker (*Flint*); Katherine Alexander (*Clare Ledge*); Priscilla Lawson (*Felice*); Mary Gordon (*Mrs. Keogh*); Donald Meek (*Reverend Flynn*); Henry Taylor (*Angelo*); Bert Roach (*Shrank*); Roger Moore (*Pianist*); Mitchell Lewis (*Orator*); Jack

Powell straightens John Beal's tie while Kennedy, Powell and Rice kibitz testily. *(Double Wedding)*

It looks like double-wedding time is approaching (dig that wreath—and Loy's outfit.) *(Double Wedding)*

Dougherty *(Chauffeur)*; G. Pat Collins *(Mounted Policeman)*.

CREDITS:

Richard Thorpe (Director); Joseph L. Mankiewicz (Producer); Jo Swerling (Screenplay); based on a Play by Ferenc Molnar; William Daniels (Photogra-

pher); Cedric Gibbons (Art Director); Frank Sullivan (Editor).

Running time, 87 minutes. Released October 1937.

ESSAY

The talented actor John Beal, who has offered many fine portrayals on screen, stage and TV over a 50-odd year career, was 27 when he found himself with Powell and Loy in one of their more amusing vehicles, the 1937 *Double Wedding*. "Bill Powell had a technique, an instinct for comedy timing that kept me in awe all through the shooting," John Beal told the author. "He was the consummate professional, never at a loss. I found my own comedy technique sharpening just from playing off him."

Based on a Ferenc Molnar play, *Great Love*, the movie was more attuned to European than American sensibilities, but as played by Powell, Loy, Beal and Florence Rice, proved itself one of the more sparkling entertainments of the year. Here Powell is a screwball

Powell and Loy decide they are made for each other. *(Double Wedding)*

painter who takes issue with prissy, stiffish clothes designer Loy's insistence on ordering everyone around to suit her own standards. When they encounter one another, Loy is trying to force her young sister, Rice, into marriage with a stuffed-shirt youngster, Beal, who despite his tender years, needs considerable loosening up to make good husband material.

The rebellious Rice, out to defy her sister, tries to initiate an affair with Powell, who has advised her to come out of her shell and try for an acting career. This enrages Loy, who is the real object of Powell's affections. After numerous hilarious complications, there is a double wedding, to which Powell lures Loy under the pretext she is attending her sister's nuptials. It takes Loy, a female equivalent of the legendary stuffed shirt of countless dramas, forever to admit she loves Powell, who has adopted heroic measures to instill some humor and flexibility in her.

Some reviewers got a mixed reaction to the film, which they thought too archly European in spots, but the public bought it, primarily due to the star power, and it was a hit because Powell and Loy, with Beal and Rice ably emulating them, made the material look better than it was. "Defrostings of the stuffy are always good for situational comedy," one critic wrote, "but if this film is a hit with the ticket buyers, it's because the stars make it seem fluid and effortless."

THE BARONESS AND THE BUTLER

1938 20TH CENTURY-FOX

CAST:

William Powell *(Johann Porok);* Annabella *(Baroness Katrina);* Helen Westley *(Countess Sandor);* Henry Stephenson *(Count Albert Sandor);* Joseph

Baroness Annabella objects to servant Powell's political career. *(The Baroness and the Butler)*

Schildkraut *(Baron George Marissey);* J. Edward Bromberg *(Zorda);* Nigel Bruce *(Major Andros);* Lynn Bari *(Klari);* Ivan Simpson *(Count Darno).*

CREDITS:

Walter Lang (Director); Darryl F. Zanuck (Producer); Lamar Trotti, Sam Hellman and Kathryn Scola (Screenplay); based on a story by Ladislaus Bus-Fekete; Arthur Miller (Photographer); Louis Silvers (Musical Direction).

Running time, 75 minutes. Released February 1938.

ESSAY

Powell did not work for four months after the death of Jean Harlow. When he did go before the cameras again, it was in Budapest, Hungary, on location shooting for *The Baroness and the Butler,* a film he was doing on loan to 20th Century-Fox. Powell had decided to retreat for a time to Europe, to get away from the sad Hollywood associations (he was not to do a film on the MGM lot for two years). Later he finished the film's interiors in Hollywood at the 20th Century-Fox studios. Laid in Hun-

Powell, the perfect butler, serves his employer, Helen Westley. *(The Baroness and the Butler)*

Annabella enjoys butler Powell's breakfast-in-bed ministrations. *(The Baroness and the Butler)*

shooting with a minimum of strain, feeling that this was the best way to ease back into harness.

Powell had not been high on the script when he read it, but it seemed the best compromise at the time. A light comedy, more than a little reminiscent of some of the situations in the 1936 *My Man Godfrey, The Baroness and the Butler* paired him with the rising new personality Annabella, for whom Darryl Zanuck (for a time) had great hopes. She would later marry Tyrone Power.

Walter Lang was assigned to direct. The script, based on a story by Ladislaus Bus-Fekete, had Powell as a butler in the home of Hungary's prime minister (Henry Stephenson), whose daughter is Annabella. The butler's post has been handed down from father to son for generations, and Powell is in complete charge of the domestic staff. There is another, political, side to him, however, and he is eventually elected to Parliament as the leader of the opposition party. Soon he is in conflict with his employer, and baroness Annabella very much resents her former butler's new role. True love conquers all, of course.

gary, the film featured shots in the Parliament Building and other locations in Budapest, which gave Powell a chance to see Europe and, incidentally, rest. He did the location

The critics seemed to find this an amusing but rather trifling conceit, though there was the usual praise for Powell's acting.

A fine supporting cast included Stephenson, Helen Westley, Joseph Schildkraut, Nigel Bruce and Lynn Bari. Only 75 minutes long, *Baroness* was no world-beater, but it was pleasant enough and served to ease Powell back into acting.

Employer Henry Stephenson is a good sport about Powell's political ambitions. *(The Baroness and the Butler)*

ANOTHER THIN MAN

1939 METRO-GOLDWYN-MAYER

CAST:

William Powell *(Nick Charles)*; Myrna Loy *(Nora Charles)*; C. Aubrey Smith *(Colonel Burr MacFay)*; Otto Kruger *(Van Slack)*; Nat Pendleton *(Lieutenant Guild)*; Virginia Grey *(Lois MacFay)*; Tom Neal *(Freddie Coleman)*; Muriel Hutchinson *(Smitty)*; Ruth Hussey *(Dorothy Walters)*; Sheldon Leonard *(Phil Church)*; Patric Knowles *(Dudley Horn)*; Harry Bellaver *("Creeps" Binder)*; Abner Biberman *(Dum-* *Dum)*; Marjorie Main *(Landlady)*; Asta *(Himself)*; Horace MacMahon *(Chauffeur)*; Bert Roach *(Cookie)*; Roy Barcroft *(Slim)*.

CREDITS:

W. S. Van Dyke II (Director); Hunt Stromberg (Producer); Dashiell Hammett (Story and Screenplay); Oliver T. Marsh and William Daniels (Photographers); Cedric Gibbons (Art Director); Edward Ward (Music); Frederick Smith (Editor).

Running time, 102 minutes. Released November 1939.

ESSAY

After two years of illness, Powell returned to a solid welcome by the studio, and later the fans, in the third of the *Thin Man* series, this one being written by Dashiell Hammett himself. Powell had to rest frequently during its making, and the studio did everything possible to facilitate his scenes with a minimum of the usual set hassles. W.S. Van Dyke, of course, was again on hand to guide the proceedings.

They look happy to be together again. *(Another Thin Man)*

Sheldon Leonard gives them the business. *(Another Thin Man)*

shepherding his own characters, could not elicit a better critical and audience reaction.

Be that as it may, there was no faulting the expert Loy-Powell performances, as well as those of a fine supporting cast, including C. Aubrey Smith, Nat Pendleton (another of his "dump cop" appearances), Virginia Grey and Ruth Hussey.

The story this time has a colonel, who fears his life is in jeopardy, inviting the Charleses for a weekend at his Long Island estate. Accompanied by baby, nurse and their dog, the perennial Asta, they show up, only to find themselves awash in a series of melodramatic

A new baby boy, William Anthony Poulsen, whose presence as Nick Jr. was merely hinted-at in the 1936 episode, is on hand this time. Fans noted that while Powell looked wan in some shots, his comic vitality was unimpaired.

While there was praise for his and Loy's performances, the critical reaction was mixed, with some reviewers commenting on the "triteness" and *"déjà vu* situations" in Hammett's screenplay. MGM, which had hired the original author, Hammett, seeking to introduce freshness into the series, was surprised that he, of all people, given the fact he was

Powell and Loy try to get to the bottom of things with Grey, Knowles and Neal. *(Another Thin Man)*

Is Grey about to spill something to the others? *(Another Thin Man)*

Has Loy embarrassed Powell with a "clue"? *(Another Thin Man)*

Playing with "Nick Jr." (*Another Thin Man*)

situations. The colonel, of course, is murdered, there is yet another murder, red herrings abound, many are suspect but few are really on top of the list. The denouement has Virginia Grey unmasked as her father's murderer. Her motive: she wanted to inherit his money.

The critics for the most part judged that *Another Thin Man* was the weakest in the series, but so popular with the public was the Powell-Loy combine that the picture grossed well.

I LOVE YOU AGAIN

1940 METRO-GOLDWYN-MAYER

CAST:

William Powell (*Larry Wilson/George Carey*); Myrna Loy (*Kay Wilson*); Frank McHugh (*Doc Ryan*); Edmund Lowe (*Duke Sheldon*); Donald Douglas (*Herbert*); Nella Walker (*Kay's Mother*); Pierre Watkin (*Mr. Sims*); Paul Stanton (*Mr. Littlejohn*); Morgan Wallace (*Mr. Belenson*); Charles Arnt (*Billings*); Harlan Briggs (*Mayor Carver*); Dix Davis (*Corporal Belenson*); Carl Alfalfa Switzer (*Harkspur, Jr.*); Bobby Blake (*Littlejohn, Jr.*); William Tannen

(*Clerk*); Ray Teal (*Watchman*); Barbara Bedford (*Miss Stingecombe*); George Lloyd (*Police Sergeant*).

CREDITS:

W.S. Van Dyke II (Director); George Oppenheimer, George Lederer, Harry Kurnitz (Screenplay); based on the novel by Leon Gordon and Maurine Watkins; Oliver T. Marsh (Photographer); Franz Waxman (Music Director); Cedric Gibbons, Daniel B. Cathcart (Art Directors); Dolly Tree (Wardrobe); Edwin Willis (Set Decorator); Douglas Shearer (Sound); Gene Ruggiero (Editor).

Running time, 99 minutes. Released August 1940.

Powell seems to be at the center of things. (*I Love You Again*)

A little tea-reading for his lady. (*I Love You Again*)

213

Loy puts a stop to Powell's nonsense. *(I Love You Again)*

Is Powell too stodgy for Loy here? *(I Love You Again)*

Powell looks dour and Loy looks bored. *(I Love You Again)*

Is Loy overly impressed with Powell's clowning? No sir. *(I Love You Again)*

214

ESSAY

Loy and Powell were together again in the 1940 *I Love You Again,* their teaming, as usual, inspiring good boxoffice grosses. And again, their old standby, W.S. Van Dyke, was on hand to guide them.

The Charles Lederer-George Oppenheimer-Harry Kurnitz screenplay has a number of convolutions which Powell, now more recovered from his severe illness and consequently more energetic, and Loy ride herd over with real panache.

In this, Loy is married to a rather stuffy, prissy gentleman, Powell, who is accidentally struck on the head and wakes up as someone else entirely. It seems (a farfetched but amusing plot twist, this) that he has been an amnesiac for a decade, and that he is actually a racy type who has lived largely outside the law and is, moreover, a womanizer of no mean attainments. Realizing that he is now rich and "respectable," with a charming wife, Powell decides to continue masking as the gentleman he has "become," until the day he can grab the money and run.

Loy's charms, of course, win him over, and soon he is deciding he may stick around a bit longer than he had originally intended to. Loy, however, has been getting sick of the

Powell tootles while McHugh and Loy burn. *(I Love You Again)*

boring gentleman she thinks she is married to, and is planning to sack him eventually. This intrigues Powell, who decides to win her all over again. This makes her suspicious, for he seems another man entirely from the one she married. When the truth emerges, she is by then sufficiently taken with him to issue a ukase Forgiving All—but by a twist of the fates, he is hit on the head yet again, and the audience is left wondering which man will emerge this time.

They are not left wondering for long, for a happy ending is presaged—and a long marriage.

The critics for the most part seemed to like this offering, with "charming," "amusing," "sparkling if mighty far-fetched," among the adjectival terms employed, and one critic opined that none of it made any sense by even minimal standards of rationality, but who cared, when Powell and Loy were strutting their stuff.

Powell keeps Frank McHugh and Loy busy. *(I Love You Again)*

LOVE CRAZY

1941 METRO-GOLDWYN-MAYER

CAST:

William Powell *(Steven Ireland);* Myrna Loy *(Susan Ireland);* Gail Patrick *(Isobel Grayson);* Jack Carson

Gail Patrick and Loy look unimpressed with Powell's pugnacious challenge to Carson. *(Love Crazy)*

Powell in drag helps Loy with her yarn. *(Love Crazy)*

A contemplative moment for the pair. *(Love Crazy)*

(Ward Willoughby); Florence Bates *(Mrs. Cooper);* Sidney Blackmer *(George Hennie);* Vladimir Sokoloff *(Dr. Klugle);* Kathleen Lockhart *(Mrs. Bristol);* Sig Rumann *(Dr. Wuthering);* Donald MacBride *("Pinky" Grayson);* Sara Haden *(Cecilia Landis);* Fern Emmett *(Martha);* Elisha Cook, Jr. *(Elevator Boy);* Joseph Crehan *(Judge);* George Meeker *(De West);* Barbara Bedford *(Secretary);* Clarence Muse *(Robert).*

CREDITS:

Jack Conway (Director); Pandro S. Berman (Producer); William Ludwig, Charles Lederer, David Hertz (Screenplay); based on their original story; Ray June (Photographer); Cedric Gibbons (Art Director); David Snell (Music); Ben Lewis (Editor).

Running time, 100 minutes. Released May 1941.

ESSAY

Though some 45 years have passed since *Love Crazy* made its debut, it still looks fresh and amusing—which says a lot about Jack Conway's well-paced direction and the entertaining inanities dreamed up by screenwriters Charles Lederer, David Hertz and William Ludwig. Some of the 1941 critics, though still enamored of Powell and Loy as a team, felt that the slapstick was carried further than usual, but pardoned the total on the grounds

Are Sidney Blackmer and Powell getting what they want from Loy? *(Love Crazy)*

ankle, with the result that she overstays her not-too-welcome welcome. Frustrated, Powell goes out for a time with Gail Patrick, a former flame who is now married.

Bates (in fine form as the mischievous, malicious type she trademarked in that era, as in *Rebecca*) proceeds to fill Loy with suspicions as to her husband's activities, so she retaliates by dallying with Jack Carson. Desperate to hold on to her, Powell, on the advice of his lawyer, feigns insanity, thus frustrating any Loy moves toward a divorce. But Loy, not to be outdone, and suspicious of his "mental illness," calls his bluff; in short order he is in the loony bin, where shrinks Sig Rumann and

of its irresistible comic feel. Conway might not have had Van Dyke's instinctive ease and fluidity when guiding his stars, but he had his own brand of professionalism, first demonstrated during their 1936 *Libeled Lady,* and he kept the *Love Crazy* action on target for the most part.

In this, Powell and Loy are about to start off their wedding anniversary with a properly suitable connubial celebration of the more intimate kind, when Florence Bates, Loy's mother, shows up. She promptly sprains her

Loy looks upset, and witchy Florence Bates looks delighted, by Powell's head problem. *(Love Crazy)*

Powell looks unamused by what these guys are doing. *(Love Crazy)*

A moment for quiet clowning. *(Love Crazy)*

Back to back, but not eye to eye. *(Love Crazy)*

Vladimir Sokoloff bumble around with him until he flees in desperation.

Back in the house, he learns that the police are out to bring him back to the sanitarium with all sirens blaring, so he proceeds to shave off the trademark moustache and go into drag posing as his twin sister. Bates, all unknowing, sends "the girls" off to bed—thus providing one of the more comical reconciliations of the year. Powell is a riot in drag—it offers him a chance to show a freshly inventive side of himself—and he delivers in fine style. Fans wrote in that they missed the moustache, though.

Powell makes Loy nervous with his balancing act. *(Love Crazy)*

SHADOW OF THE THIN MAN

1941 METRO-GOLDWYN-MAYER

CAST:

William Powell *(Nick Charles);* Myrna Loy *(Nora Charles);* Barry Nelson *(Paul Clarke);* Donna Reed *(Molly Ford);* Sam Levene *(Lieutenant Abrams);* Alan Baxter *(Whitey Barrow);* Dickie Hall *(Nick Charles, Jr.);* Loring Smith *(Link Stephens);* Joseph Anthony *(Fred Macy);* Henry O'Neill *(Major Jason I. Sculley);*

Powell and Loy, Asta and "Nick Jr." look contented here. *(Shadow of the Thin Man)*

218

A nice domestic scene. *(Shadow of the Thin Man)*

Stella Adler *(Claire Porter);* Louise Beavers *(Stella);* Will Wright *(Maguire);* Tito Vuolo *(Louis);* Arch Hendricks *(Photographer);* Pat McGee *(Handler).*

CREDITS:

W.S. Van Dyke II (Director), Hunt Stromberg (Producer); Irving Brecher, Harry Kurnitz (Screenplay); based on a story by Harry Kurnitz; William Daniels (Photographer); Robert J. Kern (Editor).

Running time, 97 minutes. Released November 1941.

ESSAY

It was back to W.S. Van Dyke again for another outing with "The Thin Man" (who, originally, of course, had been actor Edward Ellis, not Powell) and for this fourth set-to, Powell and Loy went foraging for the culprit designated by the plot in the world of athletes, bookies, gamblers and other offbeat characters.

The plot was on the slight side, and the

The pair run into a hassle with a cop. *(Shadow of the Thin Man)*

screenwriting was not first class, and some critics believed that the Powell-Loy combination in the "Thin Man" métier were getting a little thin, not because their thespic expertise

219

Powell and Loy with Stella Adler. *(Shadow of the Thin Man)*

Henry O'Neill and Barry Nelson look impressed with Powell here, but not Loy. *(Shadow of the Thin Man)*

had faltered but because the sameness of the situations and gags was beginning to pall. Dickie Hall played Nick Jr., and while he was winsomely attractive, he was not given much to do—nor was Asta.

This time, a jockey gets murdered at the race-track, followed by the murder of a newspaper reporter with a history of consorting with gamblers. Barry Nelson, another newspaperman, is held on suspicion of the murders. There are the usual red herrings and suspects who turn out to be innocent, and the windup (which most fans were not awaiting

with bated breath, so familiar was the format) reveals that the jockey died accidentally but let it appear that the same man who later murdered the reporter had actually murdered him. Kindly Henry O'Neill turns out to be the murderer of the second man (are you following this), but it takes Nick and Nora a little time to unmask him while they enjoy themselves and clown in their usual style.

As a slightly novel twist dreamed up by the screenwriters Irving Brecher and Harry Kurnitz, Donna Reed plays a gambler's girlfriend and red herring, but the audience, suspicious of her presence at first, feeling she is just interesting enough to be the real murderer, is thrown off by her eventual innocence of wrongdoing. Barry Nelson, who later won stardom on the stage, is graphic and arresting in his rather limited role.

The fine mounting, Loy's attractive gowns and Powell's never-failing panache do not result, however, in one of the series' better offerings, as the plot was meandering and at times obscure in motivation.

CROSSROADS

1942 METRO-GOLDWYN-MAYER

CAST:

William Powell *(David Talbot)*; Hedy Lamarr *(Lucienne Talbot)*; Claire Trevor *(Michelle Allaine)*; Basil Rathbone *(Henri Sacrou)*; Margaret Wycherly *(Madame Pelletier)*; Felix Bressart *(Dr. Andre Tessier)*; Sig Rumann *(Dr. Alex Dubroc)*; H.B. Warner *(Prosecuting Attorney)*; Philip Merivale *(Commissaire)*; Vladimir Sokoloff *(Carlos Le Duc)*; Guy Bates Post *(President of the Court)*; Fritz Leiber *(Deval)*; Frank Conroy *(Defense Attorney)*; James Rennie *(Martin)*.

CREDITS:

Jack Conway (Director); Edwin H. Knopf (Producer); Howard Emmett Rogers and John Kafka (Screenplay); Guy Trosper (Story); George

Powell with leads Trevor and Lamarr. (*Crossroads*)

Boemler (Editor); Songs by Arthur Schwartz and Howard Dietz.

Running time, 84 minutes. Released July 1942

Rathbone and Trevor set a trap for Powell. (*Crossroads*)

It's courttime, and Trevor looks grim while the Powell-Lamarr duo ignore her. (*Crossroads*)

Powell and Lamarr greet an oily, sinister Rathbone, who is up to no good. (*Crossroads*)

Rathbone seems to be getting what he wants from Powell and Lamarr. *(Crossroads)*

ESSAY

Someone at Metro-Goldwyn-Mayer, reputedly Louis B. Mayer himself, got the bright idea of casting William Powell with Hedy Lamarr, and it turned out well, for a change (some miscastings with Powell earlier had resulted in clashing chemistries). The beautiful Lamarr was, at that time, a notoriously weak actress hampered by an Austrian accent, and Powell was just what she needed. His mellifluous voice and poised comportment would rub off on her in some way, it was hoped, and expectations were surpassed. Lamarr, a reserved, rather wooden actress in front of the camera, despite her facial beauty and smouldering glances, seemed much more animated and sparkling with Powell.

Crossroads, the story they were given to carry, displayed Powell as a diplomat in Paris who via amnesiac experiences is led by conniving blackmailers Basil Rathbone and Claire Trevor to believe that he was formerly a thief and a murderer. Lamarr is his loyal wife who stands by him through thick and thin, and of course the conniving Rathbone-Trevor duo get their due comeuppance in time.

Jack Conway kept the action percolating along nicely. The script by Guy Trosper had been based on an original story by Howard Emmett Rogers. The pacing was fine, the acting exemplary, and the photographer made Powell and Lamarr look altogether dreamy in

222

what few love scenes they were permitted amidst the constant bursts of melodrama.

Margaret Wycherly headed a cast of sterling players, including Felix Bressart, Sig Rumann, H.B. Warner and Philip Merivale, and the sequences in which Powell seeks to trace, step by step, his journeys into his alleged "past" are limned excitingly.

From one critic: "Having sampled the likes of Robert Taylor, Spencer Tracy, James Stewart, Robert Young and Charles Boyer, Miss Hedy Lamarr has now been handed Mr. William Powell, and in his hands she seems much more assured and relaxed." Truer words were never spoken. The duo were to be teamed again by MGM.

THE YOUNGEST PROFESSION

1943 METRO-GOLDWYN-MAYER

Powell, hat and paper in hand, looks half-amused, half-alarmed as Edward Arnold carries his sleeping daughter, Virginia Weidler. Marta Linden plays the mother. *(The Youngest Profession)*

Virginia Weidler *(Jean Lyons)*; Edward Arnold *(Burton V. Lyons)*; John Carroll *(Dr. Hercules)*; Jean Porter *(Patricia Drew)*; Marta Linden *(Mrs. Edith Lyons)*; Dick Simmons *(Douglas Sutton)*; Agnes Moorehead *(Miss Featherstone)*; Marcia Mae Jones *(Vera Bailey)*; and such guest stars as William Powell, Greer Garson, Lana Turner, Robert Taylor, Walter Pidgeon.

CREDITS:

Edward Buzzell (Director); George Oppenheimer, Charles Lederer, Leonard Spigelgass (Screenplay); based on the book by Lillian Day; Charles Lawton (Photographer); Ralph Winters (Editor).

Running time, 82 minutes. Released September 1943.

ESSAY

Powell made a flashingly brief appearance as himself in one of those juvenile concoctions in which Metro-Goldwyn-Mayer, on its off days, seemed to revel. Edward Buzzell directed this so-so stuff about autograph fanatics, with Virginia Weidler as the most fanatical of them all.

Based on a Lillian Day book which had sold well (it had no serious pretensions), the Charles Lederer-George Oppenheimer-Leonard Spigelgass screenplay had to do with Weidler's assorted shenanigans among the famous, the aim being to get all the autographs the traffic—or rather the famous targets—will bear. Edward Arnold plays Weidler's hapless father, and Powell appears, newspaper in hand, in one sequence in which Arnold is carrying Weidler, weary from her constant autograph-solicitations, in an elevator. Powell looks, in this sequence, half-amused, half-alarmed, and no wonder, considering the juvenile goings-on all around him.

In *The Youngest Profession*, Powell was lost in a crowd in more ways than one, for also on hand, playing themselves as autograph targets, were such as Greer Garson, Lana Turner and Robert Taylor. Walter Pidgeon, another "drafted" star, tries to look jaunty and uncon-

cerned, but the rest have that why-did-they-do-this-to-me look.

"Tame stuff," one reviewer wrote, "and this story of Virginia Weidler's obsession with obtaining the signatures of various notables, all hailing from the Lion Studio, of course, benefits only from the brief appearances of some of the top MGM luminaries. Why did they do it? It can't have been for boxoffice insurance, as none of them are onscreen long enough to register."

Another reviewer singled Powell out for praise, writing: "Bill Powell can do more with a look or a gesture than ten other actors can do with ten minutes of mugging. What little he has to do in this juvenile jape, he does well—but why did he bother? For that matter, why did the others? And for that matter, why did MGM?"

THE HEAVENLY BODY

1944 METRO-GOLDWYN-MAYER

Lamarr sasses Powell and he doesn't like it. *(The Heavenly Body)*

Powell looks on glumly as James Craig and Lamarr start sharing an interest. *(The Heavenly Body)*

Is Powell realizing that Craig is a threat to his marriage? Yes! *(The Heavenly Body)*

Powell frightens the life out of Helen Freeman and Fay Bainter. *(The Heavenly Body)*

CAST:

William Powell *(William Whitley)*; Hedy Lamarr *(Vicky Whitley)*; James Craig *(Lloyd X. Hunter)*; Fay Bainter *(Margaret Sibyll)*; Henry O'Neill *(Professor Stowe)*; Spring Byington *(Nancy Potter)*; Robert Sully *(Strand)*; Morris Ankrum *(Doctor Green)*; Franco Corsaro *(Sebastian Melos)*; Connie Gilchrist *(Beulah Murphy)*.

CREDITS:

Alexander Hall (Director); Arthur Hornblow, Jr. (Producer); Walter Reisch, Harry Kurnitz and Michael Arlen (Screenplay).

Running time, 95 minutes. Released March, 1944.

ESSAY

The William Powell-Hedy Lamarr combination had registered so well in the 1942 *Crossroads* that they were reunited, this time in a comedy, in 1943, with the release delayed into 1944. The rather leering title, *The Heavenly Body,* referred not to Miss Lamarr's physical accoutrements (if truth be known, her face, rather than her rather flat-chested chassis, was her fortune) but to the august science of astronomy, which is Powell's profession in the movie. In fact, he takes his profession so seriously that the heavenly body—or rather heavenly face—of his wife, Lamarr, is somewhat neglected. So she languishes at home while he continues his ruminations on the stars and planets at his observatory. (Many a fan wrote in that they found this situation inexplicable, to say the least.)

Of course, handsome, manly James Craig, who has an appreciation for bodies more earthly than those that obsess Powell, is on hand for weak-tea competition of sorts, with Lamarr growing ever more vexed at her husband's indifference. A good cast including Fay Bainter, Henry O'Neill, Spring Byington and Connie Gilchrist supported the stars in various attitudes of commiseration and/or conspiracy, and Alexander Hall, who by that time had built up a reputation as a director of slick, smart comedies, had his work cut out for him trying to extract some sparks of wit from the screenplay handed him courtesy of scribes Michael Arlen, Harry Kurnitz and Walter Rcisch—good writers all, but in this case off their usual form.

Powell pulls out his zaniest tricks and his most inventive mugging in an honest effort to inject some vitality and surprise into a slight, indeed anemic, story, but all goes for naught.

One critic felt that if MGM regarded the Powell-Lamarr pairing as so potent, why did they let them down with such a weak vehicle. For which no reasonable or credible answers were forthcoming from the studio. Powell and Lamarr parted professional company permanently after this one, though again fans and critics noted that vis-à-vis Powell, Lamarr sparkled far more than she had with other stars.

THE THIN MAN GOES HOME

1944 METRO-GOLDWYN-MAYER

CAST:

William Powell *(Nick Charles);* Myrna Loy *(Nora Charles);* Lucile Watson *(Mrs. Charles);* Gloria De-Haven *(Laura Ronson);* Anne Revere *(Crazy Mary):* Harry Davenport *(Doctor Charles);* Helen Vinson *(Helena Draque);* Lloyd Corrigan *(Bruce Clayworth);* Donald Meek *(Willie Crump);* Edward Brophy *(Brogan);* Leon Ames *(Edgar Draque);* Paul Langton *(Tom Clayworth);* Donald MacBride *(Chief MacGregor);* Minor Watson *(Sam Ronson);* Anita Bolster *(Hilda);* Morris Ankrum *(Willoughby);* Arthur Hohl *(Charlie);* Connie Gilchrist *(Woman with Baby);* Irving Bacon *(Tom);* Chester Clute *(Drunk);* Don Wilson *(Masseur)*

CREDITS:

Richard Thorpe (Director); Everett Riskin (Producer); Robert Riskin and Dwight Taylor (Screenplay); from a story by Harry Kurnitz and Robert Riskin, based on characters created by Dashiell Hammett; Karl Freund (Photographer); Cedric Gibbons and Edward Carfagno (Art Directors); David Snell (Music); Ralph Winters (Editor).

Running time, 100 miuntes. Released December 1944.

ESSAY

After an absence of three years, yet another Thin Man film was brought forth, this time

Lucille Watson joins Powell and Loy in a moment of puzzlement. *(The Thin Man Goes Home)*

Enjoying a larkish moment. *(The Thin Man Goes Home)*

A nice family-gathering pose. *(The Thin Man Goes Home)*

Birthday time for Powell as Watson, Loy and Davenport look on. *(The Thin Man Goes Home)*

under the directorial aegis of Richard Thorpe (Van Dyke died the year before, 1943). This was the fifth in the series, made a decade after the original. Thorpe, competent director that he was, did not have Van Dyke's feel for the material, nor did he have Van Dyke's light touch and awareness of the Powell and Loy chemistry. The result was a pedestrian, rather dull affair.

It came out, however, in late 1944, during a spate of boxoffice prosperity for the movies. In 1944, starved for entertainment and anxious to forget the real-life exigencies of the war, the public went to movies as never before, and this latest *Thin Man* profited from the propitious times by making money. Also, the fans were glad to see the two familiar, beloved faces back strutting their stuff in roles that had become their trademark.

But some critics, more objective than the public, believed that it was time the series was laid to rest, as it had passed its prime and had lost the verve and snap that had distinguished it in the Thirties.

In this, Powell goes home (as per the title) to visit his parents, Harry Davenport and Lucile

Ed Brophy looks fazed by the goings-on. *(The Thin Man Goes Home)*

Powell shows the suspect paintings to Donald Meek, while Morris Ankrum, Donald MacBride, Tom Dugan, Leon Ames and Helen Vinson look on. (*The Thin Man Goes Home*)

It looks like Gloria de Haven is in trouble. (*The Thin Man Goes Home*)

A quiet moment on the set. (*The Thin Man Goes Home*)

Watson, in their small town, named Sycamore Springs. Davenport, playing a doctor, and Watson added much strength and solidity to the slight proceedings. There is a mystery concerning the murder of a landscape painter. Among the plot complications associated with the homicide are alleged secret plans for a propeller used for war planes. Then it turns out that one of the deceased's paintings, if rendered transparent, is replete with blueprint photostats. After much scrounging around, an old school friend of Nick's, who seems a pleasantly innocuous type, is unmasked as the culprit. "Tired" was

Powell unravels the mystery for Ed Brophy, Lloyd Corrigan and Gloria de Haven. (*The Thin Man Goes Home*)

Traveling-with-pet time for Powell and Loy. (*The Thin Man Goes Home*)

the verdict of the critics on this, and one wrote that trying to tie up Nick and Nora and their Thirties-style patter with wartime spy nonsense was a mixing of the proverbial oil and water.

228

ZIEGFELD FOLLIES

1946 METRO-GOLDWYN-MAYER

CAST:

All-star, including William Powell, as Florenz Ziegfeld, and Fred Astaire, Gene Kelly, Judy Garland, Lucille Ball, Lena Horne, Esther Williams, Kathryn Grayson, Virginia O'Brien, Victor Moore, Edward Arnold, Cyd Charisse, Keenan Wynn, James Melton, Marion Bell, *et al.*

CREDITS:

Vincente Minnelli (Director); Arthur Freed (Producer); Robert Alton (Choreographer); songs by Freed and Warren, and George Gershwin, among others; special dances by Fred Astaire and Gene Kelly.

Running time, 110 minutes. Released February, 1946.

Powell as Ziegfeld meditates, up in Heaven, on his achievements. (*Ziegfeld Follies*)

In another attempt, a rather lame one, at an "all-star" format, MGM came up, on the tenth anniversary of *The Great Ziegfeld,* with *Ziegfeld Follies.* Powell at 54 was drafted, due to his starring success in the earlier picture, into what amounted to a cameo role, as he looks down, purportedly from Heaven, at what he has wrought in various forms of musical comedy and extravaganza excellence. Aged to look even older than 54, and attired in an outfit that was half-robe, half-dressing gown, he holds a miniature follies-girl doll and walks about looking at various renditions of his old Broadway triumphs, all of them in baroquely moulded frames. Meanwhile what could be stars *or* white round spots glisten in the background.

While appreciative of the tribute to his earlier triumph as Ziegfeld, Powell was as aware as anyone of the passage of time and the changed conditions at MGM, and knew perfectly well that his role was an essentially thankless one. Indeed, at this point his star was sinking inexorably at MGM.

Vincente Minelli directed this Technicolor production, and Robert Alton choreographed. Fred Astaire, Virginia O'Brien, Lena Horne, Gene Kelly, Esther Williams, Cyd Charisse, Keenan Wynn, Edward Arnold and others all did their specialties, either in acting, singing or dancing—and of course Judy Garland particularly shone in her sketch spoofing a star who took herself too seriously. What with Esther Williams in a spectacular aquatic number, this musical—MGM's third built around Ziegfeld—didn't have a plot or need one; everyone who was anyone simply showed up and shone distinctively. Powell opens the proceedings "up in Heaven," then is seen no more.

Production on *Ziegfeld Follies* had dragged on for over a year, as numbers were staged, then discarded, and the end result, while it made money, was an empty piece of showoff, in the opinion of many critics, though there were plaudits for the work of Astaire, Garland and others. Powell took no pride in his "cameo" appearance in what was essentially a glittering, overproduced mishmash.

THE HOODLUM SAINT

1946 METRO-GOLDWYN-MAYER

Powell with leading ladies Williams and Lansbury. *(The Hoodlum Saint)*

CAST:

William Powell *(Terry O'Neill);* Esther Williams *(Kay Lorrison);* Angela Lansbury *("Dusty" Millard);* James Gleason *("Snarp");* Lewis Stone *(Father Nolan);* "Rags" Ragland *("Fishface");* Frank McHugh *("Three Finger");* Slim Summerville *("Eel");* Henry O'Neill *(Lewis J. Malbery);* Emma Dunn *(Maggie).*

CREDITS:

Norman Taurog (Director); Cliff Reid (Producer); Original Story and Screenplay by Frank Wead and

The girls' 1940-ish styles in a 1920 period piece were blatantly anachronistic. *(The Hoodlum Saint)*

Powell and Angela Lansbury are up to something here. *(The Hoodlum Saint)*

James Hill; Ray June (Photographer); Ferris Webster (Editor); Nathaniel Shilkret (Musical Score).

Running time, 91 minutes. Released June 1946.

ESSAY

Metro-Goldwyn-Mayer had initial high hopes for *The Hoodlum Saint,* and it was touted by the flacks as the picture perfectly tailored to William Powell's measure, but when it was released in June, 1946, the results, with both critics and the public, were dismal.

Many things were wrong with it. Norman Taurog, the director, did not exploit the possibilities in the material; the original story by Frank Wead was sadly deficient in wit and even sense; and, as one commentator put it, "Powell could have phoned in his performance."

Even a prime supporting cast did not help to redeem *The Hoodlum Saint.* Among the actors in attendance were such as James Gleason, Lewis Stone, Frank McHugh and Slim Summerville; all gave it their best, but the lines and situations just weren't there. Hoping to hype things up at the boxoffice, MGM commandeered Esther Williams from her swimming pool and cast her as a wealthy socialite, and Angela Lansbury was deputized to apply some paprika as a nightclub singer who warbles two ditties nicely, but the material defeated everyone.

Powell, who had felt that the story had possibilities, expressed himself later as most disappointed with the results. In the story he returns from World War I without a job. A former journalist, he comes to feel, cynically, that "the big dough is the only thing that counts." Turncoating, he goes to work for a financier he had formerly attacked in a newspaper, and fights his way to wealth. When he secures the release of an old friend, a small-time bookmaker, from a jail rap, he lets him think it was through the good offices of St. Dismas, Patron Saint of Hoodlums, the Good Thief of crucifixion legend. Later, when the crash wipes him out, Powell returns to journalism, finds himself writing of St. Dismas, gets religion, and tries to inspire his old pals

Fresh from World War I, Powell romances socialite
Williams. *(The Hoodlum Saint)*

Powell referees a Williams-Lansbury discussion. *(The
Hoodlum Saint)*

with a golden-rule philosophy. Along the way
he has romanced Williams and Lansbury. *The
New York Times* said: "Though facile and expert [Powell's] performance is not enough to
swerve this entertainment from its uneven
and dreary course."

SONG OF
THE THIN MAN

1947   METRO-GOLDWYN-
MAYER

Dean Stockwell is the new "Nick Jr." here. *(Song of the
Thin Man)*

CAST:

William Powell *(Nick Charles);* Myrna Loy *(Nora
Charles);* Keenan Wynn *(Clarence Krause);* Dean
Stockwell *(Nick Charles, Jr.);* Phillip Reed *(Tommy
Drake);* Patricia Morison *(Phyllis Talbin);* Gloria
Grahame *(Fran Page);* Jayne Meadows *(Janet
Thayer);* Don Taylor *(Buddy Hollis);* Leon Ames
(Mitchell Talbin); Ralph Morgan *(David Thayer);*
Warner Anderson *(Dr. Monolaw);* William Bishop
(Al Amboy); Bruce Cowling *(Phil Brant);* Bess
Flowers *(Jessica Thayer);* Connie Gilchrist *(Bertha);*
Marie Windsor *(Helen Amboy);* Asta Jr. as Himself;

It looks like Revelation Time, as Leon Ames and Patricia Morison look on. *(Song of the Thin Man)*

Keenan Wynn has their attention. *(Song of the Thin Man)*

Loy seems to be holding the right cards. *(Song of the Thin Man)*

Telephone time for the pair. *(Song of the Thin Man)*

Relaxing on the set. *(Song of the Thin Man)*

Tom Dugan *(Cop);* Matt McHugh *(Taxi Driver);* Morris Ankrum *(Inspector);* Jerry Fragnol *(Young Nick, Age 5).*

CREDITS:

Edward Buzzell (Director); Nat Perrin (Producer); Stanley Roberts (Story); Nat Perrin and Steve Fisher (Screenplay); based on characters created

At the gaming table. *(Song of the Thin Man)*

by Dashiell Hammett; Charles Rosher (Photographer); Douglas Shearer (Sound); Cedric Gibbons, Randall Duell (Art Decorators); Gene Ruggiero (Editor).

Running time, 86 minutes. Released August 1947.

ESSAY

This item was the sixth and last of the Powell-Loy *Thin Man* outings, as well as their thirteenth appearance together in thirteen years. (They were to be seen in one more picture unrelated to the Nick-and-Nora characters.) On hand as Nick Charles, Jr., is Dean Stockwell, and a good cast including Keenan Wynn, Phillip Reed, Patricia Morison, Gloria Grahame and Jayne Meadows tries to perk things up, but without success.

The director this time was Edward Buzzell, who had even less feel for the subject matter

The bedroom's in disarray. *(Song of the Thin Man)*

Discipline time for Nick Jr. *(Song of the Thin Man)*

than Richard Thorpe had had the previous time out. Fifty-five when he did this, Powell seemed a little tired and settled for the once-winning jauntinesses of the Nick Charles character, and at 42 Loy seemed a bit superannuated for the coynesses and inventive adaptabilities of Nora.

Powell has a question for clarinetist Don Taylor. *(Song of the Thin Man)*

Nor did Gloria Grahame seem to belong to this particular film as a nightclub singer putting over naughty songs in the best 1947 style. Keenan Wynn, an actor of a later period than the Thirties, also seemed to grate anachronistically, with his acting style in no way in sync with that of Powell and Loy.

This time, a bandleader on a gambling ship is murdered; Nick and Nora are guests at a party aboard ship. Topping the list of suspects is the owner of the ship, who had been known to quarrel with the murdered man; then he, too, is almost dispatched. As befits his portrayal, Powell is on the verge of retiring (as Nick the Detective, that is), and he only takes on the case because he is intrigued by its titillating ramifications. The suspects include the gambler who holds the murdered man's IOU, another musician who had fought with him over a woman, an agent who had fought with him over business matters, and a protective father loath to see his daughter marry the victim. Eventually the agent is declared the culprit—his wife had been up to adulterous monkeybusiness with the murdered man, thus incurring his jealous wrath.

The critical verdict on this last gasp of the series was: "Pack it in." Which Powell and Loy proceeded to do.

Powell has a relaxed time with Elizabeth Taylor and Zasu Pitts. *(Life With Father)*

LIFE WITH FATHER

1947 WARNER BROS.

CAST:

William Powell *(Clarence Day)*; Irene Dunne *(Vinnie Day)*; Elizabeth Taylor *(Mary Skinner)*; Edmund Gwenn *(Rev. Dr. Lloyd)*; Zasu Pitts *(Cora)*; Jimmy Lydon *(Clarence Day, Jr.)*; Emma Dunn *(Margaret)*; Moroni Olsen *(Dr. Humphries)*; Elizabeth Risdon *(Mrs. Whitehead)*; Monte Blue *(Policeman)*; Derek Scott *(Harlan)*; Martin Milner *(John)*; Clara Blandick *(Miss Wiggins)*; Creighton Hale *(Father of Twins)*; Nancy Duff *(Delia)*.

CREDITS:

Michael Curtiz (Director); Robert Buckner (Producer); Donald Ogden Stewart (Screenplay); based on the play by Howard Lindsay and Russel Crouse; Max Steiner (Music); Robert Haas (Art Director); Peverell Marley (Photographer); William V. Skall (Associate Photographer); George Amy (Editor). Technicolor.

Edmund Gwenn and Irene Dunne make the non-religious Powell uncomfortable. *(Life With Father)*

Running time, 118 minutes. Released December 1947.

ESSAY

The stage hit *Life With Father*, which had run up some 3,224 performances on Broad-

Dunne and Powell are hosts to visiting Taylor, who pursues their son. *(Life With Father)*

Zasu Pitts and Irene Dunne seem glad to see Gwenn, but Powell looks pained. *(Life With Father)*

Powell resigns himself to going for baptism, while Dunne looks pleased. *(Life With Father)*

Dunne and Powell in a warm, close moment. *(Life With Father)*

It looks like a family spat between Powell and Dunne.
(*Life With Father*)

are many touching and authentic details of patriarchal 1880's family life along the way, and one scene, in which the proud Clarence, who scorns all religion, is forced, albeit haughtily, to ask God for the life of his ill wife, was alone calculated to win Powell an Oscar. He was nominated for one that year, after winning the New York Critics Award, but lost to his old friend Ronald Colman's performance in *A Double Life*.

A host of fine character actors are on hand to enhance the 1880's ambience, and director Michael Curtiz directed it with enthusiastic affection. The young Elizabeth Taylor, age 15, appears as a visiting cousin, and Jimmy Lydon is a calfishly endearing Clarence Jr. Photographed in Technicolor, with a fine score by Max Steiner, lavishly produced and sumptuously mounted, *Life With Father* displays Powell as a versatile actor of consummate skill. It was certainly the height of his career, and deeply fulfilling for him, to boot.

way, featured as its centerpiece Clarence Day, the irascible, idiosyncratic, domineering but deeply human and essentially beneficent patriarch of an 1880's New York clan. Powell had wanted the role since 1942, and had begged Louis B. Mayer to buy it for him. However, Mayer felt the asking price— $500,000 plus a percentage of the gross—was much too steep to be acceptable to MGM's New York office, and refused.

The disappointed Powell was to languish for a full five years before Warner Bros. bought the story and offered him the role. It was just the lift to his career that he needed after his so-so roles at MGM, and he plunged into the part delightedly. Irene Dunne was cast opposite him, and they made a classic pair. This was no Nick-Nora stuff, but rather a touching depiction of a marriage of opposites who are bound, nonetheless, by a deep affection. Vinnie, Clarence Day's wife, as played by Dunne, is motivated throughout the picture by a single obsession, to get Powell to a baptismal font. In the end she succeeds, and the entire family rides off to the church. There

THE SENATOR WAS INDISCREET

1947 UNIVERSAL

CAST:

William Powell *(Senator Melvin G. Ashton)*; Ella Raines *(Poppy McNaughton)*; Peter Lind Hayes *(Lew Gibson)*; Arleen Whelan *(Valerie Shepherd)*; Ray Collins *(Houlihan)*; Allen Jenkins *(Farrell)*; Charles D. Brown *(Dinty)*; Hans Conreid *(Waiter)*; Whit Bissell *(Oakes)*; Norma Varden *(Woman At Banquet)*; Myrna Loy *(Mrs. Ashton)*.

CREDITS:

George S. Kaufman (Director); Nunnally Johnson (Producer); Gene Fowler, Jr. (Associate Producer); Charles MacArthur (Screenplay); based on a story by Edwin Lanham; William Mellor (Photographer); Daniele Amfitheatrof (Music); David

The Senator is a wily mountebank. (*The Senator Was Indiscreet*)

Peter Lind Hayes is unimpressed with Powell, here with Arleen Whelan. (*The Senator Was Indiscreet*)

Horsley (Special Effects); Bernard Herzbrun, Boris Levin (Art Directors); Sherman Rose (Editor).

Running time, 88 minutes. Released December 1947.

ESSAY

For her last appearance in a William Powell picture, Myrna Loy had what amounted to a cameo role; her presence was welcome, nonetheless. *The Senator Was Indiscreet* was one of Charles MacArthur's comical conceits, with a screenplay based on a novel by Edwin Lanham. George S. Kaufman directed, and Nunnally Johnson produced. The story had Powell as a monumentally stupid old senator—large with rhetoric but as phony as they come.

It seems this old humbug is hellbent on becoming President, and he goes on a self-promotional binge, promising the voters the most outlandishly unrealistic boons including the offer of free college educations. Then

Making a train-platform speech. (*The Senator Was Indiscreet*)

there is mail on tissue paper to save on expenses, three-hour work weeks for eight days' pay, among other foolish promises.

As for his rivals, he keeps them off base by hinting that he has written of all his dealings in a diary—a diary that would automatically expose their malfeasances as well as his own.

239

Allen Jenkins seems alarmed by Powell. (*The Senator Was Indiscreet*)

Powell's press agent, Peter Lind Hayes, betrays him by giving the diary to his girlfriend, newswoman Ella Raines. Raines publishes excerpts from the hot-hot diary in the paper, and Powell is forced to flee to the South Seas. That's where Loy comes in. She accompanies him into "exile," after the scandal breaks, as the "perfect wife" of legend. Loy was brought in by Universal as an "in" gag, and she had very little to do, but did it in her usual forebearing, long-suffering style as Powell's helpmate. She later told newsmen that she had accepted the role because she thought it might be fun.

"Entertaining," "biting," "hilarious" wrote the critics, and Powell's amusing performance shared equally in the reviewers' praise with Kaufman's knowing directorial touch and MacArthur's witty dialogue. According to a story of the time (late 1947), even the congressmen and senators in Washington enjoyed it, probably because they recognized the germ of truth in this amusingly iconoclastic satire. *The Senator Was Indiscreet* is considered by critics, in retrospect, as one of Powell's top-drawer performances.

MR. PEABODY AND THE MERMAID

1948 UNIVERSAL-INTERNATIONAL

Mermaid Blyth (complete with unrealistic bra and headdress jewels), spoons with a love-besotted Powell. (*Mr. Peabody and the Mermaid*)

CAST:

William Powell (*Mr. Peabody*); Ann Blyth (*The Mermaid*); Irene Hervey (*Polly Peabody*); Andrea King (*Carly Livingston*); Clinton Sundberg (*Mike Fitzgerald*); Art Smith (*Doctor Harvey*); Lumsden Hare (*Colonel Mandrake*); Fred Clark (*Basil*); James Logan (*Lieutenant*).

CREDITS:

Irving Pichel (Director); Nunnally Johnson (Producer and Screenplay); based on the novel by Guy and Constance Jones; Russell Metty (Camera); Marjorie Fowler (Editor).

Running time, 89 minutes. Released August 1948.

Andrea King tries her wiles on an unresponsive Powell. *(Mr. Peabody and the Mermaid)*

Blyth and Powell by the fish pool. *(Mr. Peabody and the Mermaid)*

ESSAY

In 1984 director Ron Howard made a comedy called *Splash* with Tom Hanks as a guy who fell in love with a mermaid, Daryl Hannah. This was not as original a theme as it appeared, for 36 years before, in 1948, William Powell and Ann Blyth had also made a film, *Mr. Peabody and the Mermaid,* directed by Irving Pichel, and this tale of a middle-aged man who falls in love with a mermaid while on a fishing vacation boasted far more grace and wit and style than the unwieldy and overlong *Splash* could ever have begun to summon.

Of course with Powell to lend distinction, style and his unique brand of wit to what was and is essentially a rather outlandish tale, the results were bound to be better than average, and while some of the critics of 1948 had reservations about it and felt Powell was wasting his abilities, it did fairly well with the public, considering the inroads of television as of that year.

Anyway, when Powell catches mermaid Blyth, he takes her home and puts her into a fishpond. To suit the still-vigilant Production Code, the mermaid's tail takes care of her lower half, while her bosom manages to get

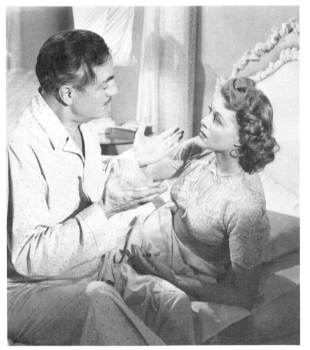

Powell tries to explain his feelings to perplexed wife Irene Hervey. *(Mr. Peabody and the Mermaid)*

covered by blankets, a makeshift bra, or anything else handy. Irene Hervey, as Powell's land-based wife, is mighty exasperated by his infatuation for this lady from the sea, and leaves him—for a time. Director Irving Pichel did better in the first half than in the second, doing what he could with the tongue-in-cheek

241

Wife Hervey wants to know what Powell is doing with that feminine garment. *(Mr. Peabody and the Mermaid)*

stuff until things ran downhill. The overall result was still a bright enough comedy, with fey overtones, and Ann Blyth matched Powell's comic moods very well, making her creature straight out of wonderland even "human" at times, if human was the word for it. Everything in time gets down to earth, or rather back to land, with Nunnally Johnson's screenplay capturing the comic values of the original—a novel by Guy and Constance Jones. Hervey, Clinton Sundberg, Fred Clark and Lumsden Hare lent able support.

TAKE ONE FALSE STEP

1949 UNIVERSAL-
INTERNATIONAL

CAST:

William Powell *(Andrew Gentling)*; Shelley Winters *(Catherine Sykes)*; Marsha Hunt *(Martha Wier)*; James Gleason *(Gledhill)*; Dorothy Hart *(Helen Gentling)*; Jess Barker *(Arnold Sykes)*; Felix Bressart

242

(Professor Morris Avrum); Sheldon Leonard *(Pocciano)*.

CREDITS:

Chester Erskine (Director); Irwin Shaw (Screenplay), based on his novel; Frank Planer (Photographer); Russell Schoengarth (Editor).

Running time, 94 minutes. Released June 1949.

ESSAY

One critic gave it as his opinion that *Take One False Step* couldn't seem to make up its mind if it were melodrama or frivolous comedy, and I, after viewing it on television a year ago, tend to agree. Again Powell plays a sleuth, though in this case an impromptu, amateur one. He starts the film as a married, highly respectable college professor who is trying to get a stuffy philanthropist to endow a new college. In the midst of these staid goings-on, a flashy flame, Shelley Winters, appears from the past, first dating a reluctant Powell, then disappearing.

It appears that Winters has been murdered, so Powell, frantic to save his reputation, and with the endowment deal on tap, chases off by

Flashy Shelley Winters leads Powell on a merry chase. *(Take One False Step)*

It's cocktail time, and Winters pours on the charm.
(*Take One False Step*)

Marsha Hunt and Powell look askance at Winters' maneuverings. (*Take One False Step*)

car from L.A. to San Francisco to decipher her fate. He encounters numerous red herrings and false alarms, before getting to the bottom of things, into the clear, and home to his wife and endowment plans.

The combination of raw, vivacious Shelley Winters and William Powell was a fan draw, and a peppery pair they made, with his insouciance balancing nicely off her brash directness. Director Chester Erskine did the best he could and Irwin Shaw's script worked well at providing lines and situations for Powell that recalled the bright material of his 1930's era. But critics and public were lukewarm.

Some of the flip dialogue seemed more appropriate to farce than the kind of ominous melodrama the scripter and director seemed to be attempting to get across, and Powell, at 57, was getting a bit frayed around the edges for the frantic hurryings, scurryings, journeyings and assorted expenditures of energy that would have taxed a man fifteen years younger. However, he gave it his best college try, and it was not his fault that the result was neither fish nor fowl nor good red herring—though of red herrings (of the wrong kind) there were plenty.

Powell holds the address book while Hunt telephones. (*Take One False Step*)

Powell sees talent in Drake. *(Dancing in the Dark)*

Menjou, Powell and Stevens plan strategy. *(Dancing in the Dark)*

DANCING IN THE DARK

1949 20TH CENTURY-FOX

CAST:

William Powell *(Emery Slade);* Betsy Drake *(Julie);* Mark Stevens *(Bill Davis);* Adolphe Menjou *(Crossman);* Randy Stuart *(Rosalie);* Lloyd Corrigan *(Barker);* Hope Emerson *(Mrs. Schlaghammer);* Walter Catlett *(Joe Brooks);* Jean Hersholt and Sid Grauman *(Themselves);* Frank Ferguson *(Sharkey).*

CREDITS:

Irving Reis (Director); George Jessel (Producer); Mary C. McCall, Jr. (Screenplay); based in part on the musical revue *The Bandwagon* by George S. Kauffmann, Howard Dietz and Arthur Schwartz; Harry Jackson (Photographer); Songs by Howard Dietz and Arthur Schwartz; Alfred Newman (Musical Direction). Technicolor.

Running time, 92 minutes. Released December 1949.

ESSAY

At 20th-Century-Fox in 1949, Powell at 57 got an interesting part in a story about Hollywood, *Dancing in the Dark.* Directed by Irving Reis and produced by George Jessel, from a screenplay by Mary McCall, Jr., the plot had Powell, twenty years before an acclaimed star, finding himself in 1949 down-and-out and forgotten. Adolphe Menjou, a studio executive who had known him in better days, signs him up as a talent scout, feeling he will have the knack of persuading a Broadway star, who has been holding out on movies, to sign up.

Meanwhile Powell has met up with an unknown, Betsy Drake, and decides she has the talent to essay the role the studio wants the star for. Menjou and Company are reluctant about this, but change their minds when it emerges that Drake is Powell's long-lost

A man-to-man talk between Powell and Stevens. *(Dancing in the Dark)*

Powell in white tie and tails puts on the dog at the opening. (*Dancing in the Dark*)

IT'S A BIG COUNTRY

1951 METRO-GOLDWYN-MAYER

CAST:

William Powell *(Professor)*; Fredric March *(Papa Esposito)*; Gary Cooper *(Texas)*; Keefe Brasselle *(Sergeant Klein)*; Nancy Davis *(Miss Coleman)*; Gene Kelly *(Icarus)*; Van Johnson *(Rev. Adam Burch)*; Marjorie Main *(Mrs. Wrenley)*; George Murphy *(Callaghan)*; Lewis Stone *(Sexton)*; Ethel Barrymore *(Mrs. Brian Riordan)*; and S.Z. Sakall, Janet Leigh, Leon Ames, Angela Clarke, Sharon McManus, Elizabeth Risdon and Bill Baldwin, James Whitmore.

CREDITS:

John Sturges, Richard Thorpe (director of Powell-Whitmore segment); Clarence Brown, Charles Vidor, Don Hartman, Don Weis, William A. Wellman, (Directors); Dore Schary and Robert Sisk (Producers); Helen Deutsch, Dorothy Kingsley, Isobel Lennart, Allen Rivkin, William Ludwig, George Wells, Dore Schary (Screenwriters); John Alton, William Mellor, Joseph Ruttenberg, Ray June (Photographers); Johnny Green (Music Supervisor); Ben Lewis, Frederick Y. Smith (Film Editors); Douglas Shearer (Sound); based in part on stories by Edgar Brooke, Ray Chordes, John McNulty, Claudia Cranston, Joseph Petracca, Lucille Schlossberg.

Running time, 90 minutes. Released December, 1951.

ESSAY

It's a Big Country, the brainstorm of MGM production head Dore Schary, was another of those all-starrers, but this time with a special angle. It proposed to highlight the American Way of Life in a number of episodes, with stars to match. Originally, there were nine episodes. Later these were cut to seven, and in Britain only six were shown.

daughter. Of course there are misunderstandings between Powell and Drake, and she almost abandons her big chance, but eventually takes on the assignment—and shines brilliantly, of course. Along the way she forgives her father, and romances Mark Stevens.

The musical in which Drake appears is *The Bandwagon,* and some of the Arthur Schwartz-Howard Dietz songs are used. The musical-within-a-musical original, of course, was the inspiration of George S. Kaufman, Dietz and Schwartz. Big things were expected of Betsy Drake in this film, but she somehow lacked the vivacity, poise and general charisma to deliver. It was Powell's picture all the way, and he was toughly poignant as an actor once on top and now on the bottom, who has learned some harsh lessons along the way. Mark Stevens, Menjou, Lloyd Corrigan, Hope Emerson and Walter Catlett helped things along, and director Reis kept the pace fast and breezy.

The public responded to this in languid fashion and the reviews were only so-so, though Powell won personal kudoes for his sincere efforts to pump adrenaline into a limp and not-too-original story.

James Whitmore belabors Powell with train-trip gab. (*It's a Big Country*)

Powell, in his first MGM appearance in four long years, was a passenger on a train who just wants peace and quiet and his book; he is belabored by a garrulous James Whitmore, whose non-stop conversation annoys him increasingly. Powell's barely-patient looks and body movements while enduring the boring and irritating onslaught of Whitmore gab are worth seeing in themselves, and the scene is a masterpiece of "reactive listening." Whitmore later said that playing off Powell was one of his best lessons in acting, and that Powell's inventive reactions to him enhanced his own performance immeasurably. The sequence was directed by Richard Thorpe. At age 59, Powell was in fine form here. Sporting glasses, poring over a book the importunate and brash Whitmore won't let him read, he conveyed quiet exasperation in a masterly manner.

The other segments involved such as Keefe Brasselle and Marjorie Main, an unlikely pairing directed by Don Weis; Fredric March and the future First Lady Nancy Davis, directed by Don Hartman; Janet Leigh, Gene Kelly and S.Z. (Cuddles) Sakall, directed by Charles Vidor; Gary Cooper, directed by Clarence Brown; Ethel Barrymore, Keenan Wynn and George Murphy, directed by John Sturges; and Van Johnson and Lewis Stone, directed by William A. Wellman. March was an Italian-American (complete with accent) who balked at buying eyeglasses for his son; Brasselle was a wounded Korean vet who brings a letter to the mother of a soldier who died in action (best of the vignettes, according to critics); Van Johnson a minister who gets to visit the President, and so forth. Critical enthusiasm for the most part was lukewarm, and little has been heard of *It's a Big Country,* for all Schary's praiseworthy, but unwieldy, patriotic intentions, in the thirty-five years since its release.

246

TREASURE OF LOST CANYON

1952 UNIVERSAL-
INTERNATIONAL

Powell, Tommy Ivo and Rosemary DeCamp discuss matters.
(*Treasure of Lost Canyon*)

Tommy Ivo (left) is comforted by uncle, Powell, aunt
Rosemary DeCamp, Julia Adams and (in background)
Charles Drake. (*Treasure of Lost Canyon*)

CAST:

William Powell (*Doc Brown*); Julia Adams (*Myra
Wade*); Charles Drake (*Jim Anderson*); Henry Hull
(*Lucius*); Rosemary De Camp (*Samuella*); Tommy
Ivo (*David*); Chubby Johnson (*Baltimore Dan*); John
Doucette (*Gyppo*).

CREDITS:

Ted Tetzlaff (Director); Leonard Goldstein (Pro-
ducer); Emerson Crocker and Brainerd Duffield
(Screenplay); based loosely on Robert Louis
Stevenson's *The Treasure of Franchard*; Russell Metty
(Photographer); Milton Carruth (Editor); Joseph
Gershenson (Music); Technicolor.

Powell and Tommy Ivo get the goods. (*Treasure of Lost
Canyon*)

Running time, 82 minutes. Released February
1952.

ESSAY

Many of Powell's friends and associates
wondered why, at age 60, he had undertaken
to do the weak-scripted *Treasure of Lost Canyon*,

247

which, despite some handsome California locations and a cast of competent supporting players, came and went almost unnoticed by the 1952 audience. The critics gave a collective shrug on this, with damning-with-faint-praise observations like "pleasant," "wholesome," "family-trade-oriented" proliferating among the reviews across the country.

On loan to Universal for this one (MGM gave Powell little to do in the early 1950's), Powell tried his best to inject some vitality and pertinence into a limp tale, based very loosely on Robert Louis Stevenson's *The Treasure of Franchard*, which dealt with an orphaned lad, Tommy Ivo, being fleeced of his estate by crooked San Francisco attorney Henry Hull, then being given a home by his kindly farmer-doctor uncle and aunt, Powell and Rosemary DeCamp.

Next on the agenda is a complicated underwater search for an ancient treasure chest which allegedly contains valuables of considerable monetary worth. Brainerd Duffield and Emerson Crocker's screenplay then takes Powell and Ivo, under the somewhat distracted and uneven direction of Ted Tetzlaff, through assorted vicissitudes culminating in the usual homespun happy ending.

Universal made a half-hearted attempt to sell *The Treasure of Lost Canyon* across the country as an alleged "perfect picture for children to see with their parents, for the enjoyment of the whole family," but the net result was a torpid boxoffice return and frequent placings on double bills—lower half, that is.

The scenery and some fancy Technicolor helped, but not much. Powell reportedly took the role because it was wholesome and inoffensive enough, and was the best of lean pickings that year. Rosemary DeCamp, as his wife, Julia Adams, Hull, John Doucette, Chubby Johnson and Charles Drake gave sincere performances, but *Treasure of Lost Canyon* belongs near the bottom tier of Powell film releases.

THE GIRL WHO HAD EVERYTHING

1953 METRO-GOLDWYN-MAYER

CAST:

Elizabeth Taylor (*Jean Latimer*); Fernando Lamas (*Victor Y. Raimondi*); William Powell (*Steve Latimer*); Gig Young (*Lance Court*); James Whitmore (*Charles "Chico" Menlow*); Robert Burton (*John Ashmond*); William Walker (*Julian*); Paul Harvey (*Senator Drummond*); Emory Parnell (*Auctioneer*); John McKee (*Secretary*); Earle Hodgins (*Spotter*).

CREDITS:

Richard Thorpe (Director); Armand Deutsch (Producer); Art Cohn (Screenplay); based on the novel *A Free Soul* by Adela Rogers St. Johns and the play by Willard Mack; Cedric Gibbons, Randall Duell (Art Directors); Andre Previn (Music); Helen Rose (Costumes); Paul Vogel (Photographer); Ben Lewis (Editor).

Running time, 69 minutes. Released June 1953.

ESSAY

Powell's final appearance for Metro-Goldwyn-Mayer was in *The Girl Who Had Everything*. It was his second go-round with the young Elizabeth Taylor, then 21, who had played, at 15, with Powell in the 1947 *Life With Father*. The film was a remake of *A Free Soul*, the 1931 Adela Rogers St. Johns story that had been one of the big hits of that year with Norma Shearer, Clark Gable, and Lionel Barrymore, who won an Academy Award for his role in it.

Powell, though listed third in the billing after the popular young combination of Taylor and the then-fast-rising Fernando Lamas, has the strong Barrymore part—that of a

Taylor, suitor Gig Young, and attorney dad Powell seek some recreation. *(The Girl Who Had Everything)*

Taylor and Powell in a tense moment. *(The Girl Who Had Everything)*

Lamas and Powell square off as Taylor looks on ruefully. *(The Girl Who Had Everything)*

by slapping Shearer around in one scene. Lamas, while hardly up to Gable's *homme fatale* standard, and moreover afflicted with a thick Spanish accent, managed to project lots of 1953-style sex appeal nonetheless, and Taylor, though only 21, managed a fair approximation of Norma Shearer's reckless, spoiled rich girl who thinks it a thrill to be in love with a criminal, only to be speedily disillusioned.

Art Cohn did a considerable rewrite of the 1931 version, eliminating strong courtroom scenes in which Barrymore had shone, and otherwise rearranging things for the changed

criminal lawyer involved with the lawless, who disapproves of his daughter's relationship with arch-criminal Lamas, played in 1931 by Clark Gable, who had achieved his initial fame

249

Taylor looks worried as Powell and Lamas quarrel. *(The Girl Who Had Everything)*

Lamas menaces Powell in a tense scene. *(The Girl Who Had Everything)*

tastes of the 1950's. Nonetheless Powell, in his strongest role of his final years in films, registered with telling impact as he tries to warn Taylor off Lamas, then takes on the criminal to save his daughter. Lamas is conveniently rubbed out by rival gangsters headed by low-key but deadly James Whitmore, and contrite Taylor and relieved Powell are reconciled. Richard Thorpe as director did what he could

with the material. The 1953 critics praised Powell but felt that the film was at best only a fair remake of a sizzling 1931 original. Gig Young played the "good-guy" suitor of Taylor originated in 1931 by Leslie Howard.

HOW TO MARRY A MILLIONAIRE

1953 TWENTIETH CENTURY-FOX

CAST:

Lauren Bacall *(Schatze Page);* Marilyn Monroe *(Pola Debevoise);* Betty Grable *(Loco Dempsey);* William Powell *(J. D. Hanley);* Cameron Mitchell *(Tom Brookman);* Fred Clark *(Waldo Brewster);* Rory Calhoun *(Eben);* Alex D'Arcy *(J. Stewart Merrill);* David Wayne *(Freddie Denmark).*

CREDITS:

Jean Negulesco (Director); Nunnally Johnson (Producer); Nunnally Johnson (Screenplay); based on plays by Zoe Akins, and Dale Eunson and Katherine Albert; Joe McDonald (Photographer); Alfred Newman (Music); Cyril Mockridge (Incidental Music); Louis Loeffler (Editor); Cinema-Scope and Technicolor.

Running time, 95 minutes. Released November, 1953.

ESSAY

Powell was not exactly at the center of the action in this remake of the amusing 1932 film, *The Greeks Had a Word for It.* The plot dealt with three girls (Lauren Bacall, Marilyn Monroe and Betty Grable) on the make for men and money, preferably via the rich-husband route. Monroe winds up with her landlord (David Wayne) who is having tax problems. Grable is at first marooned in a mountain cabin by a lecherous married man

(Fred Clark) but is rescued by a handsome forest ranger (Rory Calhoun). Bacall at first decides to marry elderly Texas millionaire Powell for his money, though she really loves a young man (Cameron Mitchell) whom she thinks is poor, therefore ineligible for marriage.

All is straightened out at the end, with Mitchell revealing his wealth, Powell gracefully conceding to True Love, and all getting married.

More than one critic pointed out that Powell helped lift this essentially indifferent comedy to a sophisticated and knowing level. At 61, his talent undiminished and his suave way with the ladies as intact as ever, Powell dominated the scenes in which he was in, and got everyone reacting to him on-screen in a way that raised the over-all acting standard.

He is maturely understanding and patient with the indecisive Bacall, whom he knows to have a good heart beneath her mask of opportunism, and he joshes delightfully with Monroe and Grable. An actor who had appeared with the top film stars of his era, after over 30 years in the business, Powell found himself in scenes with newer stars like Bacall, Monroe

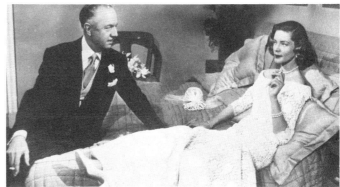

Powell and Bacall have a heart-to-heart talk. *(How to Marry a Millionaire)*

Monroe and Grable react to Powell's gifts, but Bacall is indifferent. *(How to Marry a Millionaire)*

Powell obviously admires the Monroe charms, even in glasses. *(How to Marry a Millionaire)*

Monroe and Grable await their grooms as Powell looks on. *(How to Marry a Millionaire)*

251

and Grable, who had been children or teenagers at the time of his greatest stardom. One reviewer noted that Powell, involved with this battery of feminine star-power circa 1953, seemed to round out his years of onscreen romancing nicely.

Produced in CinemaScope and Technicolor, *HTMAM* was produced by Nunnally Johnson and directed by Jean Negulesco. Johnson's screenplay gave Powell some bright lines, which he delivered with his usual feeling for timing and nuance.

MISTER ROBERTS

1955 WARNER BROS.

CAST:

Henry Fonda *(Lieutenant Roberts);* James Cagney *(Captain);* William Powell *(Doc);* Jack Lemmon *(Ensign Pulver);* Ward Bond *(C.P.O. Dowdy);* Betsy Palmer *(Lieutenant Ann Girard);* Phil Carey *(Mannion);* Nick Adams *(Reber);* Harry Carey, Jr. *(Stefanowski);* Ken Curtis *(Dolan);* Frank Aletter *(Gerhart);* William Henry *(Lieutenant Billings);* Pat Wayne *(Bookser);* Tige Andrews *(Wiley);* Jim Moloney *(Kennedy).*

CREDITS:

John Ford, Mervyn LeRoy (Directors); Leland Hayward (Producer); Frank Nugent and Joshua Logan (Screenplay); based on the play by Thomas Heggen and Joshua Logan and the novel by Thomas Heggen; Winton C. Hoch (Photographer); Art Loel (Art Director); Jack Murray (Editor). CinemaScope. WarnerColor.

Running time, 123 minutes. Released August 1955.

ESSAY

Powell's final film part—his last role in any medium—was as the philosophical, laid-back medic "Doc" in the screen version of the phenomenal stage hit *Mister Roberts.* He more

than held his own in a cast that included Henry Fonda, as Mister Roberts, who wants to get off the plodding Navy supply ship to see some real action in World War II; James Cagney, as the feisty Captain; and Jack Lemmon, in an Oscar-winning performance in a supporting role as Ensign Pulver, the cut-up who is always hatching hare-brained schemes.

Mister Roberts had run into a number of production problems, and the indisposed John Ford was replaced, late in the shooting, by Mervyn LeRoy. There were also numerous snags during the location shooting in Hawaii; and by the end of production, Powell decided he was bone-tired, and wished to retire permanently.

His "Doc" is a quiet, self-effacing, paternal figure, and, as written, is no match for the more high-pressure histrionics of co-stars Fonda, Cagney and Lemmon, but nonetheless Powell makes something special of it, and later told friends that it was an admirable movie—and role—to go out on.

Experienced and world-weary, Doc has been everywhere and done everything, and life holds no further surprises for him. As

Powell, Fonda and Lemmon are up to something. *(Mister Roberts)*

Lemmon gets all bubbled-up while Powell and Fonda watch. (*Mister Roberts*)

Lemmon asks Powell to join him in some hi-jinks. (*Mister Roberts*)

Can alchemist Powell do the trick? Fonda and Lemmon want to find out. (*Mister Roberts*)

board. Resorting to his medicine cabinet, Powell's expressions and movements are hilarious as he applies iodine and other substances to the original mixture to produce the alcoholic effects desired. The life on the supply ship underlines the futility, waste and essential madness of war itself, and Powell's character helps underline the ambience expertly. His was truly "a role to go out on."

subtly played by Powell, he conveys via gestures and expressions the essence of his character, and many of the critics singled him out for special praise in a picture which was a smash hit and won a 1955 Academy Award nomination.

Powell has a special opportunity to shine in a scene where he helps the intrepid and brash Lemmon to transform what he calls "white lightning" into Scotch so that Lemmon can use it to seduce a nurse who is temporarily on

Fonda, Cagney, Powell and Lemmon on the set. (*Mister Roberts*)

PORTRAITS

William Powell (signature)

254